The End of the State

Andrew Levine

VERSO
The Imprint of New Left Books

First published by Verso 1987

Verso, 6 Meard Street, London W1

Typeset in Times Roman by
Leaper & Gard Ltd, Bristol, England

Printed and bound by CPI Group (UK) Ltd,
Croydon, CR0 4YY

British Library
Cataloguing in Publication Data

Levine, Andrew
The end of the state.
1. State, The
I. Title
320.1′01 JC11

ISBN 978-0-86091-881-3

Contents

Preface 1
Introduction 9

Part 1
1. Rousseau's State 25
2. Rousseau's Politics 39
3. Rousseau and Revolution 50
4. Revolution and Utopia 67

Part 2
Prelude 87
5. Historical Materialism 92
6. Socialism 106
7. The Socialist State 131
8. Communism and the State 154
Conclusion 176
Notes 182
Index 197

Preface

Philosophers who endorse Marxian positions, as I shall, are bound to appear oppositional. What follows goes against some powerful currents of thought in ways that are peculiarly ironic and, it will appear, anachronistic. Perhaps it cannot be otherwise where Rousseauean positions figure prominently.

My aim is to investigate the possibility of replacing coercive political arrangements with cooperative associations of individuals and groups. In the past decade and a half, cooperation has become an important topic for social philosophers and political theorists. In the same period, the influence of Kantian moral philosophy has declined in favor of utilitarianism and contractarian theories of Hobbesian inspiration. Cooperation has been a concern mainly of neo-Hobbesian contractarians[1] and utilitarians.[2] My subject, however, is the very different sort of cooperation Kant called membership in a 'republic of ends' (*Reich der Zwecke*). Rousseau provided a vocabulary in which the difference can be succinctly put: for Hobbes and his successors, cooperation is a contrived coordination of private wills; in the Kantian view (which is also Rousseau's), cooperation is a consequence of the preeminence of a general will. The meaning of this distinction and its implications will become clearer in what follows. It will suffice for now to say that membership in a republic of ends is based on peoples' common interests as autonomous beings; not, as in Hobbesian and utilitarian accounts, on interests derived from what distinguishes one individual from another empirically.

It is not quite that Kantianism has fallen into general disfavour, but that it again has flourishing rivals. In philosophy, as in many human undertakings, allegiances shift as expectations give way to disappointments. Where alternative positions are relatively fixed and few, as they are in moral philosophy, and where no position is ever likely to defeat its rivals entirely, a cyclical movement is predictable. In all likelihood, then, Kantianism will someday recoup; perhaps it will even recover its hegemonic place. But that day is not yet. A similar, cyclical movement has been described for political activism and public involvement.[3] In these terms, in comparison with a decade and a half ago, the present period is evidently a quiescent phase, a time of retreat into private life. Arguably, these swings of the pendulum are related. It is a theme of what follows that the republic of ends has — or can be made to have — revolutionary political implications. Rival views of cooperation, particularly those of Hobbesian inspiration, typically have a different political cast. Neo-Hobbesians conceive cooperation through bargaining. Their ideal order is the marketplace. It is not surprising, therefore, that the burden of their work in the theory of cooperation, insofar as it draws political conclusions, tends to favour a status quo largely organized through (capitalist) markets and their supporting institutions. This political motivation is vague and certainly less important for shaping actual views than internal, philosophical considerations. But it is worth noting that contemporary treatments of cooperation, when not expressly apolitical, are more likely to be conservative and procapitalist than socialist and revolutionary.

It is worth noting too that after a brief renaissance coincident with the last major phase of political activism and Kantian influence in political and moral philosophy, political philosophy itself has been in decline. Political philosophers have become moral philosophers: the theory of the state and of politics has devolved into a theory of the foundations of political philosophy and of morality. I would not gainsay this shifting emphasis. It has plainly been constructive. But it too has abetted the decline of Kantianism in political thought. Despite its enduring appeal, Kantian moral philosophy is painfully obscure in contrast to its rivals. For philosophers concerned with rejecting obscurity, it is tempting to try to make do without Kant, particularly when the terrain has shifted from expressly political matters (where

Kantian obscurities are not so evident) to more fundamental philosophical concerns (where they are).

In any case, what follows here goes against the grain again in focusing, as Rousseau did, on the state and politics, leaving underlying moral philosophical foundations largely aside. My goal, like Rousseau's, is to defend a certain vision of ideal arrangements by exhibiting its cogency. I intend neither to defend this vision directly against alternative views nor to investigate its foundations. This book is mainly an essay in political philosophy; indeed, in Rousseauean political philosophy, modified to accord with defensible and relevant Marxian views on history and the state.

I therefore address the question of cooperation and its prospects almost exclusively in its political dimensions, and from a moral philosophical standpoint nowadays in partial eclipse. Apart from references to Hobbes and occasional uses of 'game' theoretic devices, what follows may therefore seem only marginally concerned with work on rational cooperation. However this impression is misleading. I have chosen to intervene in current discussions obliquely, to gain a better purchase on cooperation than can be achieved from a more direct engagement. I hold this conviction despite, and even because of, the tendency of rival treatments.

I will maintain that, despite all that distinguishes Marx's theoretical orientation from Rousseau's and Kant's, Marx envisaged communism as an earthly republic of ends. Indeed, my principal objective will be to argue in support of the Marxian vision of a stateless social order under communism. This too goes against the current, even within contemporary Marxism. In the past decade and a half, along with a general decline in left-wing politics, the Left, including that portion of the Left that continues to identify with Marxism, has become less visionary and less inclined than ever to take communism seriously. The widespread identification of communism with Communism, the political and economic system in force in existing socialist countries, is partly to blame. But it is appropriate here to note a particularly ironic reason for communism's decline: the influence of some of the most progessive social forces to have arisen in advanced capitalist countries in recent years. Specifically, the ecological movement and the women's movement have implicitly and (usually) inadvertently raised doubts about the vision I want to defend. These movements are likely components in any future struggle for communism. Yet each has abetted the decline of communism as an ideal.

The struggle against environmental degradation and for care and stewardship of natural resources is, of course, in no way opposed to communism. But the resurgence of interest in environmental concerns during the 1970s and 1980s has been motivated, in part, by a neo-Malthusian belief in the material limits of economic growth. The rationale is familiar: with finite resources, there is presumably a physical limit on how much can be produced, even with the introduction of new technologies. If that limit is within sight, as some environmentalists contend, and if population continues to grow, as seems inevitable, then economic expansion will become increasingly impossible. Individuals will therefore have to be satisfied with less. But, as we shall see, abundance — or its near approximation — is a prerequisite for communism. If abundance is impossible, then communism is impossible too. I shall not directly confront this challenge here nor shall I consider the extent to which ecological concerns can be excised from claims about limited resources. I would simply assert what I shall go on to assume: there are no material limits to growth of a sort that would make communism impossible; and that ecological concerns are indeed detachable from the worries that nowadays sometimes motivate them. Nothing that follows here hinges on the latter claim. However if the former assumption proves unsustainable, communism will become accordingly more problematic and therefore communist statelessness will too.

The women's movement, in turn, has fostered theoretical orientations that, in varying ways, impugn ideals like communism that seem to accord insufficient attention to expressly feminist concerns. For the present, I would only acknowledge the existence of this genre of criticism; and note its irony. In view of the complexity of the issues feminism raises, it would be impossible, except at great length, to address feminist challenges to social and political theory generally and, specifically, to communism as an ideal. At the risk of seeming naïve or worse to allies in the women's movement, I would assert the conviction that it is also unnecessary. It will be helpful, however, in view of objections that will inevitably be raised, to make the stance I shall assume explicit.

The burden of most feminist research in political philosophy has been to identify and fault past and current political theory (including Rousseau's and Marx's) for its *de facto* exclusion and outright derogation of women. These findings are incontrovertible and important. But however infirmed Rousseauean political philosophy and Marxism may be by partiarchal attitudes, it remains to show how there is more to do than correct for (sometimes considerable) insensitivities and, in Rousseau's case, plain misogyny. I am not convinced that feminist critics have *shown* anything more devastating; and I doubt that they can, despite frequent claims to the contrary. I doubt, in other words, that feminism can legitimately ask for more than gender neutrality; and I doubt whether the implementation of this eminently reasonable demand has quite the far-reaching implications sometimes imputed. In any case, all that matters for the project I am about to undertake is the idea of communism; and, to my knowledge, feminist critics have yet to propose plausible grounds for thinking the communist vision itself infected by patriarchal attitudes or gender-specific conceptualizations. This possibility seems sufficiently unlikely that I think it fair to pass the burden of proof on to those who claim otherwise.

In what follows, I argue that class divisions constitute a systemic impediment to realizing the republic of ends on earth. I do not argue that there cannot be other systemic impediments; but this claim is implicit. Feminists who maintain that gender divisions are like class divisions will therefore take issue with my argument and perhaps also with its conclusions. In Marxian theory, class divisions are privileged in consequence of their role in a theory of historical change. Feminism, I would hazard, has no rival theory. The subordination of women surely is a pervasive fact of human history. However, it remains to show how, if at all, this fact shapes history's trajectory. It is pertinent to note in this regard that gender is only one of a number of salient and longstanding divisions among human beings — nationality and race are others — and that with regard to these divisions, philosophers have also characteristically derogated or ignored subordinate groups. Rectification is plainly in order here too but, again, there are no apparent implications for the subject of this book. It is one thing for a form of subordination to endure trans-historically and something else again for it to figure in an account of history's structure and direction.

It should go without saying that the view that class but not gender divisions play an explanatory role crucial for defending communist statelessness is compatible with the view that gender relations cannot be explained by class divisions and also with the claim that gender divisions are explanatory in many contexts. What I suppose is only that gender does not compete with or supplement the role I will ascribe to class and that there are no gender-based systemic impediments to communism. This is not to say that the struggle against the subordination of women and its ramifications are unimportant in the struggle for communism. Quite the contrary. Whatever detracts from full equality and the autonomy of persons is an obstacle in communism's way and should be opposed by all necessary political and extra-political means. Indeed, I will argue that transforming human nature is the central political task for socialist societies in the transition to communism. The subordination of women is surely a major obstacle to be fought against in the course of this generalized transformation.

In the present work I continue themes I have pursued elsewhere. My treatment of Rousseau expands upon but also corrects what I first attempted ten years ago in *The Politics of Autonomy*;[4] and my continuing interest in this genre of argument is explained, in part, by the criticisms I have levelled against its principal, contemporary rival in *Liberal Democracy*.[5] More pertinently, this book is, in large part, an elaboration of some suggestions advanced in the final chapter of *Arguing for Socialism*.[6] This overlap involves occasional references to works in which I have more fully defended claims I also advance here. However, I have tried in all cases to provide enough in the way of background elaboration and argument for this book to stand entirely on its own.

Among the (too few) positive changes in the intellectual climate of the past decade and a half, I would ascribe pride of place to the emergence of an analytical current of thought among philosophers and social scientists concerned with Marxian themes. In contrast to the opacities and outright obscurantism that have long afflicted western Marxisms, clarity and argument have come to be valued; and programmatic posturing has given way to a theoretical practice that aims at drawing sound and insightful distinctions and providing conceptual structure. What follows draws heavily on some of these achievements, especially G.A Cohen's reconstruction and defence of historical materialism[7] and John Roemer's analysis of exploitation in Marxian theory.[8] Beyond this debt, I have endeavoured to continue their commitment to clarity and their dedication to assert no more than can be supported; but also to reclaim as much of traditional Marxism as can be defended.

It has become clear, more than a century after the fact, that very little Marx wrote can be endorsed without qualification. But Marx did provide a theoretical orientation that remains viable and timely. It will become clear in what follows that, for investigating the possible futures of the state, Marxian theory is indispensable; not least for the powerful support it lends to hope for a genuinely free and humane future.

An ancestor of chapter 3 appeared in *The Canadian Journal of Philosophy*, vol. 8, no. 3, September 1978, under the title 'Robespierre: Critic of Rousseau'; and Chapter Five derives substantially from a paper I wrote with Elliott Sober called 'What's Historical About Historical Materialism?' published in *The Journal of Philosophy*, vol. 82, no. 6, June 1985. I am grateful to the editors of these journals for permission to draw on this material. Portions of this book, in earlier incarnations and in various permutations, were given as lectures at the University of Arizona, the University of Southern California, the University of Calgary and the Graduate Center of the City University of New York.

Many friends and colleagues have helped shape my ideas on the end of the state and, in one way or another, affected what is to follow. I owe particular thanks to Nanette Funk, Elisabetta Galeotti, Kai Nielsen, Carole Pateman, Joel Rogers, Robert Ware and Terry Winant for suggestions and comments. Elliott Sober was, as noted, co-author of a close predecessor of Chapter Five. He has also been a valued friend and nagging philosophical conscience for all the years we have been colleagues. Joshua Cohen, Jane Mansbridge, Heda Šegvić, Michael Walzer and Erik Wright read part or all of earlier drafts of this book and provided comments in heroic detail. With this level of criticism and support, there should be no need for the ritualistic assumption of responsibility by the author for the flaws and inaccuracies that remain. But, for better or worse, I have persisted stubbornly in resisting certain criticisms and evading others; and must acknowledge responsibility accordingly.

I should add, in fairness, that on the question of state autonomy under socialism — and the related issue of the character of existing socialism — a number of the individuals just cited have views very different from my own. The brief Note that concludes Chapter Seven constructs a composite criticism of my position, based on some of the questions they have raised. My aim there is not so much to add to the arguments already adduced as to clarify points of contention. There is plainly more to be said on these subjects — and also on many of the antecedent claims that underlie and motivate my stance. But, for reasons to be explained in course, views opposed to mine, even if adopted, need not undo my principal conclusions in defence of the end of the state. In any case, a more sustained investigation of the issues in dispute must await a different time and place.

I am grateful to the Graduate School at the University of Wisconsin-Madison and to the Wisconsin Alumni Research Fund for material support during the early stages of this project, and to the National Endowment for the Humanities which indirectly paid part of my salary through an institutional grant to the Institute for Advanced Study in Princeton, where I was a member for the 1985-6 academic year. By far the major part of the writing, revising and niggling — and also much of the thinking and discussing — that has gone into making this book took place during that year at Princeton. I cannot sufficiently thank the Institute and its staff for their support and for providing a truly outstanding environment for intellectual work.

Introduction

The idea of communism — the inspiration for generations of socialist militants and the guiding principle of Marxian theory and practice — today seems naïve at best, a vestige of an untenable and outdated optimism. But there is more to the old idea than nowadays appears. I shall not quite defend communism here. To do so would require consideration of many empirical, historical and theoretical issues that I will not even broach; and speculation on institutional arrangements that I will not attempt. What follows is, however, a step towards a defence of communism. It is a philosophical brief for taking the idea seriously. For reasons that will emerge in course, the principal focus will be on politics and political theory and, since communist societies are, in the traditional view, stateless, on the end of the state. It is this feature of communism, perhaps its most problematic aspect, that is my subject.

As a first approximation, stateless societies are societies without public coercive institutions, where individuals behave freely and cooperatively, without recourse to the use or threat of force. In its vision of a stateless future, Marxism therefore joins anarchism.[1] What follows, then, is both an investigation in Marxian political theory and an examination of the cogency of the anarchist vision. Orthodox Marxists and anarchists will not endorse all that is to follow. However the conclusions I draw are very much in accord with the spirit, if not the letter, of these doctrines. To most readers, therefore, what follows will seem an essay in utopianism. It is indeed, if that term is taken to connote support for a vision of ideal, but possible, political (or extra-political) arrangements. Here 'utopianism' will be used in a different way: to connote support for the impossible. In this sense, 'utopian' is an accusation of considerable gravity. To be utopian is to promote unrealizable objectives; and, by doing so, to encourage political ventures likely to lead to ruin. What is and is not utopian will be in contention throughout what follows. I will maintain, in opposition to what nowadays seems plain, that communism — and therefore anarchism (or some close approximation) — is *not* utopian; that, quite the contrary, it is a viable ideal that ought to guide political practice.

To reflect on communism is necessarily to reflect too on socialism and on revolution. Socialism will refer here to economic systems that, like capitalist economies, recognize no economically relevant juridical or customary social divisions but that, unlike capitalist economies, disallow private ownership of society's principal means of production.[2] Revolution will designate fundamental transformations in basic social or political institutions. It is not necessary, according to this definition, that a revolution be abrupt, only that it be radical. Indeed, I will argue that communism can only be brought to fruition by a process that is both revolutionary and protracted. The political economy of socialism and the dynamics of revolutionary change will therefore be very much in contention throughout what follows. However political philosophy and socialist theory will, for some time, be kept distinct. It will be convenient to develop bearings in political philosophy before situating states in economic systems. Socialism will therefore remain in the background until Part 2. Revolution will be a principal concern, expressly or implicitly, throughout.

That political institutions today are, in large part, consequences of the social and political revolutions of the past is beyond serious dispute. That the present age is itself an age of revolutionary change is more problematic. If ours is indeed an age of revolution, then political theory ought to incorporate an understanding of the revolutionary unheavals that develop, alter and overthrow political forms and practices. On the other hand, if fundamental institutional change is an affair of the past, it may be appropriate to conceive the state and revolution separately; and even to read revolution out of political philosophy altogether. Contemporary political philosophy tends implicitly towards this latter view. Political philosophy is widely acknowledged to be *about* historically variable forms, but *not* about transformations of these forms. The present work assumes, instead, that an understanding of revolutionary processes is essential for understanding on-going political life; and that the state *and* revolution, not just the state, is the proper subject of political philosophy.

In this respect and in others too, what follows is in fundamental accord with Marxian views of politics and society. But the philosophical perspective I shall adopt derives, in the main, from Rousseau. As in *The Social Contract,* my concern will be with ideal political arrangements, with what is possible 'taking men as they are and laws as they might be'.[3] I will argue that the conclusions Rousseau drew, in reflecting on this concern, are essentially right; and I will agree with Rousseau on a wide range of substantive issues. I think Rousseau erred seriously only when he lapsed into utopian speculations as a political economist and philosopher of history — domains where Marx's thought, properly qualified and elaborated, provides a remedy. Rousseau's political philosophy, though anachronistic, is generally sound. My intent, therefore, is to *correct* Rousseau by incorporating defensible and pertinent Marxian positions into a philosophical framework of Rousseauean provenance. I am convinced that Rousseau's political philosophy provides the best and perhaps the only point of departure for upholding the vision communists and anarchists share.

A philosophical theory of politics is necessarily at some remove from actual politics and from strategic, historical and sociological reflections on politics. Rousseau was particularly insistent on distinguishing political philosophy from other kinds of political theory, sharply contrasting normative political philosophy from positive political science.[4] As noted, political philosophy, in Rousseau's scheme, investigates 'laws as they might be', taking 'men as they are'. Political science investigates actually existing laws and institutions. *The Social Contract,* Rousseau declares, is an exercise in normative political philosophy. Its aim, he tells us, is to construct a theory of the *de jure* state — of political arrangements that exist in right — regardless of their existence in fact. Actual political communities, *de facto* states, are therefore not Rousseau's subject.[5] In drawing this distinction, Rousseau suggests a division between what is and what ought to be that recalls the 'utopian socialisms' Marx inveighed against and that contradicts the Hegelianism Marx never entirely overcame. Thus Marx could hardly identify with the project of *The Social Contract.* Still, in a very general way, Marx too recognized a distinction between normative and descriptive theories of the state. He did intimate a vision of ideal social (classless) and political (stateless) arrangements and, despite what is sometimes claimed, he was not averse to appealing to normative standards for assessing societies and states. Of course, Marx was, in Rousseau's sense, a descriptive political scientist too: providing accounts of political communities that already exist or have existed, and advancing claims about the constraints past and present conditions impose on future political arrangements. Normative and descriptive concerns are intermeshed in Marx's reflections on the state in capitalist societies and in his speculations on the political forms to be established after capitalism. Still, ideal political arrangements are a legitimate concern even from a Marxian point of view. Indeed, if I am right, a normative focus is indispensable for defending communism itself and therefore, in very large part, for motivating Marxian theory and practice.

Following Rousseau's lead, then, the objective here will be to investigate the *idea* of the end of the state and, for reasons that will become apparent, the theory of the socialist state and its possible futures. In this regard, existing socialist states and their futures are largely irrelevant. Rousseau held his account of the *de jure* state subject only to the constraint that it 'take men as they are' — that it accord, in other words, with basic facts about human nature and the human condition. To that eminently reasonable constraint I would add — more by way of precision than supplement — the constraint of historical possibility. These constraints will be specified here through thought experiments in the manner of contractarian political philosophy. Needless to say, a more complete account of human nature and the human condition and of historical possibility *would* require more careful attention to pertinent historical evidence, including the experience of existing socialism, and would require a fuller account of social psychological factors as well. In Chapters Seven and Eight, where the transformative effects of democratic participation become an issue, the limitations of the method I employ will become evident; and it will be necessary to take some plausible (but disputable) claims about human psychology and group dynamics essentially on faith. However my aim, like Rousseau's in *The Social Contract*, is only to show the idea of communist statelessness coherent and applicable in principle, 'taking men as they are and laws as they might be'. It is not to discuss the actual prospects for communism. Given my much more limited and tractable objective, contractarian thought experiments are eminently appropriate, even if they are in principle vulnerable to correction in the light of empirical findings. With this proviso 'let us therefore begin', as Rousseau would have it, 'by putting aside all the facts, for they have no bearing on the question'.[6]

On the whole, Marxists have tended to follow Marx in disparaging Rousseau and disavowing any intellectual debt to him.[7] But there has also been a counter-current. What follows here stands very much on the shoulders of a few eminent Western Marxists who did acknowledge and utilize the deep conceptual affinities joining Rousseau and Marx. My understanding of Rousseau's political philosophy has been shaped, in part, by Louis Althusser's lectures on *The Social Contract*,[8] and my sense of Rousseau's importance for Marxian political theory has been enhanced by the writings of Galvano Della Volpe[9] and Lucio Colletti.[10] For Colletti, there is no Marxian political theory distinct from Marxian appropriations of Rousseauean themes. It will be evident that I reject this sweeping assertion, though I support the general outlook it conveys. *Pace* Colletti, the juxtaposition of Rousseau's thought with Marx's is useful for identifying distinctively Marxian contributions to political theory. At the same time, Marxism provides a vantage point from which the understanding of Rousseau's political philosophy can be advanced, its limitations specified, and its continuing relevance for understanding politics appreciated.

There are conceptual affinities joining Rousseau and Marx that will receive scant attention here; and others that will not be noted even in passing. The focus will be on aspects of their respective views that bear on the idea that, in principle, states can cease to be necessary for coordinating individuals' behaviours; that, in Saint-Simon's words which were adopted by Engels, 'the governance of men' can give way to 'the administration of things'. This notion, unacknowledged by Rousseau and only very equivocally endorsed by Marx, is central to the political theory of both. The idea is tellingly, though misleadingly, expressed by a number of metaphors standard in the Marxian tradition. The most celebrated of these is, of course, the withering away of the state. Another is the Hegelian idea of the *Aufhebung* of the state, its transcendence or supercession. In what follows, I shall use these metaphors as seems appropriate. It should be born in mind, however, that these expressions are used *only* metaphorically, that they cannot plausibly be taken literally and that they are even ostensibly opposed.

What is left after the state withers away or is finally superceded is, again, what Kant would call a republic of ends; an association of persons moved by a single will, the general will which is the true will of each associate. The republic of ends in Kantian thought is a regulative idea: a vision of moral agents interacting harmoniously through the internalized compulsion of reason itself. To examine the end of the state philosophically is therefore to investigate the republic of ends politically; to determine what, if any, relevance this notion might have for political life. I will maintain that Rousseau 'discovered' the republic of ends[11] and that Marx, in turn, demonstrated its historical possibility.

Rousseau's aim in *The Social Contract* was to establish the coherence and possible applicability of the idea of *de jure* political authority. He neither argued for nor identified its presuppositions, but only intimated what Kant and others would later explore. Similarly, the central concern here will be solely with the viability of the republic of ends as a political ideal. I shall say very little about its desirability and virtually nothing about the philosophical commitments that motivate its communist and anarchist proponents. Autonomy was indisputably what Rousseau valued most, and it is among the commitments that motivated Marx.[12] The arguments expressed here, however, do not depend strictly on a commitment to autonomy in Rousseau's sense. Arguably, Marx's paramount concern was self-realization, the actualization of human potentialities.[13] It would therefore seem that Rousseau and Marx were not of one mind. For Rousseau, autonomy is a trans-historical, indeed essential, human trait. For Marx, at least after his critique of Feuerbachian essentialism in *The German Ideology* and the *Theses on Feuerbach*, self-realization is not an essentialist notion. In Marx's view, human capacities, needs and wants, though materially constrained, are historically specific and continually developing. Were my subject the anthropological foundations of the political vision Marx promoted, I would want to argue nevertheless that autonomy and self-realization are not nearly so distinct as may appear. However I will not attempt that argument here. For the present purpose, the differences and similarities are, in any case, unimportant. Whatever it is that makes the end of the state desirable, it is only the coherence and possible applicability of the idea that is my concern. This study respects Rousseau's boundary between political philosophy and moral theory, and seldom ventures into the latter domain. What follows therefore begs the fundamental questions in just the way *The Social Contract* did. Rousseau's example shows that this deliberate limitation can often be productive.

Readers of Rousseau will appreciate the difficulty — and artificiality — of reconstructing Rousseauean positions in unequivocal, straight-forward expositions. And students of Marxism will recognize the obstacles in the way of extracting the intention of Marx's writings — not so much in consequence of their equivocations or obscurities, but because they are difficult to encounter directly, having become virtual palimpsests overlaid with "authoritative" interpretations serving polemical ends. Similar considerations hold for the other authors treated here: for Lenin and Robespierre and even, in lesser degrees, for Tocqueville and Burke. It would be foolhardy, therefore, to set forth in this contested terrain with the expectation of finding univocal philosophies to reconstruct and develop. I therefore readily concede that the interpretatations I will advance are liable to well-founded dispute. I am not so much concerned, however, with representing views definitively as with engaging Rousseau and Marx — and also Robespierre, Burke, Tocqueville, Lenin *et al.* — as collaborators and antagonists in the ongoing investigation of the issues they and those who have taken them to heart have brought to the fore.

Historical accuracy is, of course, a *desideratum*, even if definitive interpretations must remain elusive. But this study is only incidentally an investigation in intellectual history. If I focus on Rousseau and Marx and the others it is not so much because of an interest in them *per se*, but because there is no more direct way to investigate the vision communism and anarchism share. Rousseau and Marx — and also Robespierre, Tocqueville, Burke and Lenin — lived in what is already a distant past. But on the question of the state and revolution — and the possibility of realizing a republic of ends on earth — they still provide the best point of departure. Allowing for their anachronisms and the particularites of their respective situations, their work *can* be engaged constructively, with as much — indeed, with greater — justification than more contemporary treatments.

There is another reason too for the focus I have adopted. Inasmuch as a strictly philosophical investigation of the end of the state must leave so many questions unanswered or only partially addressed, there is some justification *faute de mieux* for identifying with theoretical traditions that support the conclusions philosophical arguments can only partially sustain. Appeals to authority — or rather to the considered opinions of great thinkers — do not substitute for the empirical and theoretical work that remains to be done. But neither are these appeals to be despised: for the orientations they suggest and the corroborations they provide. I would not want to draw any general metaphilosophical conclusions from this consideration. I do doubt that future developments in philosophy will ever render the greatest philosophical thinkers superfluous to ongoing philosophical debates. But there are philosophical problems on which progress has been made and where it is reasonable to expect determinate answers. I therefore venture no speculations about how in general philosophy should use its past. I would maintain only that for this investigation at this time, Rousseau and Marx must remain at center-stage.

How substantive views are presented is always, in some degree, a *political* judgment, and nowhere more so than where Marx is involved. What I will conclude about the state and its futures derives from views plausibly attributed to Marx. Even so, the positions I will defend could be expressed in a different voice: more remote from and perhaps even in opposition to their Marxian lineage. That I have chosen instead to emphasize the connection with Marx and to discount opposing strains of Marxian thought is a considered judgment: a deliberate identification with an *oppositional* tradition in theory and practice — and with a diffuse, but vital current within that tradition — that, for over a century, has led the struggle for communism.

As noted, this book is divided into two parts: the first focuses on Rousseau and his critics, establishing bearings in political philosophy; the second adjusts those bearings to pertinent Marxian insights about history and the state. It is not until Part 2 that specifically Marxian themes are finally introduced in Marx's name.

The historical Rousseau was not, on balance, pro-revolutionary and neither did he contemplate dispensing with states. But he provided strong reasons for drawing contrary conclusions.

My aim in Part 1 is to liberate the pro-revolutionary elements of Rousseau's thought from their uneasy coexistence with opposing views and to investigate their limitations. Chapter 1 raises the question of the end of the state from the perspective of Rousseau's political philosophy.[14] I will argue that there is a tension — indeed, a fundamental equivocation — in Rousseau's idea of the state. Retrospectively, this equivocation takes on a special significance, making Rousseau a harbinger of Marx's vision of statelessness under communism. The rest of Part 1 probes the limits of Rousseau's political theory by investigating its practical political implications. Chapter Two examines some of the measures Rousseau himself proposed for actual and imagined political communities, in order to gain a purchase on his concept of politics and its limitations. Chapter Three continues this investigation by considering radical Jacobin uses of Rousseau. I draw there on some speeches of Maximilien Robespierre — a champion of Rousseau but also an unwitting and incisive critic. Rousseauean politics is manifestly utopian and unsuited for revolutionary applications. But its flaws are instructive and its underlying principles, despite their limitations, are insightful. Chapter Four then exposes some conceptual affinities joining Rousseauean political philosophy with the conservatism of Alexis de Tocqueville and Edmund Burke, two of the most incisive critics of the French Revolution. I will maintain that there are important insights conveyed in conservative doctrine; and that these insights can be disengaged from the anti-revolutionary politics Tocqueville and Burke endorsed. In a sense, historical materialism and the Marxian theory of the state complement lines of thought the conservatives and also Rousseau pioneered. Ironically, to defend communism philosophically, conservatism must be 'stood on its feet' and deployed to counteract the utopianism that threatens revolutionary endeavours.[15]

What will emerge from these chapters is a considered view of politics generally and of revolutionary politics; a view of considerable merit and timeliness, but encumbered by difficulties and limitations. Some of these shortcomings can be rectified along Marxian lines. What Rousseau's political philosophy needs in order to avoid utopianism and liberate the insights it (retrospectively) anticipates, is precisely what Marx sought to provide: a theory of history's fundamental divisions and direction, and an account of the role of the state in historical change.

Chapter Five examines Marx's theory of history, historical materialism, explicating its substantive claims and also, so far as possible, redressing what appear to be its unsubstantiated explanatory pretensions. Chapter 6 investigates socialism — and also communism, the end of the historical trajectory Marx depicted — in light of Marxian theory; and Chapter 7 examines the role of the state in socialism, focusing on the role of democracy in the struggle for communism. In Chapter 7, I propose a view of democracy's transformative powers, based on Rousseauean views about politics; and I reexamine the traditional idea of the dictatorship of the proletariat, proposing a radical reconstruction, consonant with a certain strain of thought within classical Marxism, but at odds with Marx's own view, so far as it can be discerned, and opposed to the various understandings of the vast majority of Marxists. Chapter Eight resumes the investigation of the republic of ends and the question of utopianism, attempting to determine what, if anything, in the communist vision can be put on the historical agenda.

Finally I argue for an anarchy less anarchic than communist and anarchist doctrine sometimes suggests; but an anarchy nevertheless. Needless to say, this conclusion should not be construed as support for anarchism as a political theory or guide to practice. Anarchists confound ultimate objectives with means for achieving these objectives, failing to recognize how states (of a certain sort) are indispensible for statelessness. In the end, anarchists are utopians even if the vision they endorse actually is sustainable. But there is a way to retrieve this vision without succumbing, as anarchists do, to utopian snares. My goal is to discover how.

In order to make my case for the end of the state plausible, it will be necessary to devote considerable attention to background issues. There is some danger, then, of losing sight of the whole in the details and digressions. Let me state as succinctly as I am able, then, my overall position.

I hold that Rousseau simultaneously advanced two distinct conceptions of the state: as an association of persons grounded in legitimate violence; and as an association of persons coordinated through the rational will of each individual. The former view has a long and continuing history in western political theory; the latter conception — of the state as a republic of ends — is novel and anticipates Marx's notion of a communist society without a state. In the former sense, the state uses violence against its members to forge unity: it coordinates behaviours through the use or threat of force. Where there is a republic of ends, the state in the former sense would, of course, disappear. But public, coercive force need not 'wither away' completely. Even a state not based on force might use force against its members to overcome a collective weakness of will, manifest in the resistance of some of its members to rational self-determination. The repressive state apparatus would, in all likelihood, be diminished, but not extinguished; even as the state, in the traditional understanding, is 'superceded'.

I go on to argue that the limitations of Rousseau's thought are evident in the politics it supports. I find that Rousseau lacked an adequate concept of history and therefore of historical constraints on political undertakings. More specifically, Rousseau lacked a concept of class and class struggle. Marxian theory provides the requisite concepts. In doing so, it effectively historicizes the two concepts of the state which coexist ahistorically in *The Social Contract.* In class societies, states are unequivocally based on force: the state is the means by which a collective will, grounded in class inequality and domination, is constituted. However, after Marx, we can see that it is materially possible to move beyond class society. And, after Marx and Rousseau, we can conceive how political institutions might be concocted to implement this possibility. A state based on the exercise of the general will is a utopian fantasy so long as class divisions remain but, since history makes class divisions dispensable, it makes this kind of state — or non-state — possible too.

The republic of ends that terminates the historical materialist line of possibilities might, like Rousseau's state, have occasional recourse to force. It would do so, moreover, for just the reason Rousseau indicated: to overcome the recalcitrance of its members. What distinguishes it from historically preceding states, then, is not quite the absence of force, but the fact that it is not based on force, that its collective will is genuinely free.

Rousseau was biased towards smallness and simplicity. His ideal was a city-state composed of yeoman farmers and artisans. Presumably, communist institutions, so far as possible, should incorporate a similar bias. But, after the industrial and social revolutions necessary for making the republic of ends a political ideal, it will not be easy to retrieve very much of what Rousseau was able to take for granted. In any case, readers expecting a blueprint for a communist future will be disappointed by this discussion. I shall have nothing to say about how work will be organized or productive enterprises coordinated after 'the governance of men' has given way to 'the administration of things'. And I shall have virtually nothing to say about relations between political entities. Rousseau could safely ignore both problems. From an eighteenth-century perspective, production and distribution in the *de jure* state could proceed in the way it would under illegitimate political institutions; and political entities would be sufficiently self-contained and independent that their interactions could be few and unproblematic. But these issues cannot be evaded if, as I maintain, the *de jure* state is possible only in communist societies — with forces of production massively developed and social life organized on a global scale.

The problem of coordinating political entities is particularly acute when, as is inevitable in radical democracies, individuals are simultaneously members of different and overlapping communities, each united by a general will. As a member, say, of a neighbourhood and also of a factory, an individual might have, as it were, more than one general interest. It is tempting to conjure this problem away by appealing to an ideal consensus on ends that somehow harmonizes potential conflicts. But this 'solution' is too facile, even if it points in the right direction. There is also the related problem of combining associations into ever-larger entities, as is unavoidable if there is to be coordination on a scale appropriate for communist or even capitalist societies. It is natural to say that larger decision-making entities should take precedence over smaller and more particular units, but also that, so far as possible, direct democratic forms should be retained.

I shall suggest that these questions are best addressed in the course of an on-going political and social practice bent on achieving communism and the end of the state. In this instance, I shall agree with Tocqueville and Burke on the dangers inherent in theorizing in disregard of actual political life and, by implication, the futility of attempting to theorize about political processes that do not yet exist. But this too is less a solution than a platitude of Rousseauean inspiration waved in the direction of a genuinely vexing problem.

This book is not about the institutional implementation of communism. Its subject is communist statelessness as an ideal. I venture that somehow communism can be implemented, even if the way is not readily apparent now, and that men and women actually can organize an earthly republic of ends.

Part 1

1
Rousseau's State

The Social Contract develops a theory of sovereignty (supreme political authority) and investigates its implications. This chapter examines the theory Rousseau produced, focusing on its paradoxical structure and an equivocation that is a condition for its plausibility. These flaws are fatal. Eventually, the equivocation must be resolved and the paradox removed. But my intent here is not so much to criticize Rousseau's theory as to explicate some of its central features. Despite its shortcomings, Rousseau provided nearly all the elements required for thinking about and defending the end of the state. In a sense, the paradoxical structure of his account of sovereignty even renders the theory more useful: not least, we shall see, for its susceptibility to revision in light of the politics it suggests.

It will be helpful to distinguish two strains of Rousseau's thought: a proto-Kantian and a non-Kantian component, and, since Rousseau's theory of sovereignty is largely an affair of the Kantian component, to investigate the implications and limitations of Rousseau's Kantianism. But my concern, again, is only incidentally with the historical connections joining Rousseau, Kant and Marx. My aim is to investigate the end of the state and its replacement by a republic of ends; an idea Rousseau implicitly discovered, Kant identified and elaborated, and Marx effectively proposed as a political objective.

Two Components of Rousseau's Political Thought

In Rousseau's view, the social contract, the foundation of political association, is necessary and sufficient for establishing a society capable of sustaining moral agency — the one essentially human capacity. Politics is therefore an indispensable basis for a distinctively human existence. Thus Rousseau appears to be one of those philosophers for whom human beings are 'political animals' whose very humanity is realizable only through political association.[1] For Rousseau, however, unequivocal characterizations are seldom entirely adequate and this case is no exception.

The idea that politics is necessary for a truly human life is sometimes deemed 'classical' in consequence of its role in Aristotelian political philosophy and in Athenian political life during the classical period. Its historical rival is the 'Christian' view formulated by St Augustine in the fourth century and resumed, since the seventeenth century, in a variety of secular guises. According to this alternative conception, politics is one of many necessary evils visited upon humanity in consequence of Original Sin. Politics is essential for insuring civil order ('the peace of Babylon') and limiting the devastation human beings would otherwise bring upon themselves (culminating in Hobbes's 'war of all against all'), but it is an affliction nevertheless. For Augustine, humanity's destiny is the salvation of the elect and the damnation of the reprobate; the separation, beyond earthly time, of the City of God from the City of the Devil. By having distanced ourselves through Sin from God, the source of Being, we have become radically incapable of salvation through our own endeavours. Therefore no human activity — and certainly no political activity — can affect our destinies. If salvation is to come, it can only be through unmerited grace. Augustine's secular descendants — including Hobbes, whose sense of human depravity and incapacity for good rivals Augustine's — generally offer a less sombre prognosis for whatever they take to be the secular analogues of salvation. Early liberal theorists, for example, sought 'salvation' through commerce and were optimistic about its prospects. But commerce, in the liberal conception, takes place in non-political civil society outside the state. In effect, politics remains, even for them, among the curses of Adam — a burden it is well, wherever possible, to excise from ordinary life.[2] Of course, it cannot be excised entirely. We cannot do without politics; and it is desirable that our political affairs be conducted well. Thus liberalism characteristically relegates governance to professional politicians who pursue politics as a career, structured along lines that mimic other vocations and propelled by incentives prevalent in the society politicans superintend. Hobbes and his successors, like their intellectual forebears, often accorded extraordinary prerogatives — sometimes even absolute power — to those who govern. But, no matter how it is compensated, governance is still, in their view, a necessary evil — an ineluctable and unnatural burden on all concerned.

Rousseau denied this derogation of politics and separation of the state from society. The *de jure* state founded by the social contract *is* civil society in the form made necessary and possible by the antagonisms of the state of nature. At the same time, however, what the social contract establishes does distinguish society from the state — and even valorizes society to the detriment of the state. This understanding is fundamental to a Kantian reading of Rousseau. Kant's vision of a fully moral order is not a state in the traditional sense; it is an internally coordinated republic of ends. In terms of the distinction Augustine and his successors draw, it is a social, not a political, order — a community, like the City of God. It is not organized through force, as earthly Cities are, but on self-legislated principles of practical reason, Kant's secular analogue to Augustinian love for the divine. To the extent Rousseau anticipated this Kantian idea, he too conceived 'salvation' — in this case, the realization of moral agency — *socially*, not *politically*, as an affair of society, not the state.

Rousseau's affinities with Kant have already been noted and will be elaborated more fully below. But Rousseau's Kantianism comprises only one aspect of his political philosophy. Rousseau *was* indeed proto-Kantian, but not exclusively so. This is one important reason, among others, why in reflecting on the state and revolution and on the possibility of a stateless future, Rousseau's express views are not in all respects like-minded or even consistent. In *The Social Contract* and elsewhere, there is no single notion of politics nor an unequivocal anticipation of the idea of the end of the state but two, relatively distinct conceptions, only apparently connected systematically. It is these strains of Rousseau's political philosophy that I call its Kantian and non-Kantian components.

To identify these components and distinguish them, it is neither necessary nor apt to focus directly on Kant's moral and political philosophy. It will suffice to consider Rousseau's own positions and their implications. What follows therefore compares Rousseau not with Kant but with himself: distinguishing the exponent of Kantian views of autonomy, authority, obligation and rational agency from the political thinker for whom what matters is politics itself as a fundamental human pursuit, regardless of the moral vision it may suggest. The Kantian Rousseau is classical in depicting the social contract as the basis for a fully human life and Christian in separating society from the state. Indeed, insofar as the *de jure* state passes into a republic of ends, the Kantian Rousseau loses hold of the political altogether. On the other hand, the non-Kantian Rousseau is classical in assigning pride of place to politics but, as we shall see in Chapter Two, as Christian as any liberal in conceiving commerce as a sphere apart from and prior to the state. The non-Kantian Rousseau is, in any case, the premier theorist of the specificity and variability of actual politics. Thus at the same time — or, more precisely, in the same texts — Rousseau submerges politics in an apolitical moral vision, and grasps the essence of political life with unparalleled perspicacity. Any attempt to find consistency in Rousseau's thought is therefore bound to founder. Rousseau's reflections on politics are too often at cross purposes. It is well, therefore, to disjoin the Kantian from the non-Kantian components of Roussauean political philosophy, at least initially, and to reflect separately on each. The Kantian component will be mainly at issue here; the non-Kantian component in subsequent chapters.

Rousseau's Kantianism

'The fundamental problem of political philosophy,'Rousseau announces, 'for which the social contract provides the solution' is 'to find a form of association which defends and protects with all common forces the person and goods of each associate, and by means of which each one, while uniting with all, nevertheless obeys only himself and remains as free as before.'[3] The 'form of association' individuals in a state of nature seek to constitute is, Rousseau insists, a state that obligates its associates by establishing a supreme authority or sovereign over them. The sovereign has the might to protect 'the person and goods of each associate'. But its authority does not derive from this force. The sovereign commands by right. It does so, Rousseau insists, insofar as the individuals who collectively constitute the sovereign through the social contract obey only themselves, that is, insofar as they remain free. The freedom of which Rousseau speaks, then, is not the freedom of the state of nature. Outside states, one is free to the extent one is not restrained by others in the pursuit of one's ends. It is therefore impossible for individuals in a state of nature to find themselves, as Rousseau would have it, 'forced to be free'. What matters for authority and obligation is autonomy. Autonomy is not, like natural freedom, an absence of restraints, a freedom incompatible with laws. On the contrary, autonomy implies subordination to laws, but laws of one's own legislation. Laws obligate us if and only if, by making them, we obligate ourselves.

Rousseau construes this requirement literally. For autonomy to be realized citizens must actually legislate. Voting in popular assemblies, indeed, the method of majority rule, is 'a consequence of the contract itself'.[4] But direct democratic choice is not sufficient for realizing sovereignty. What the social contract entails is disinterested voting. The social contract, Rousseau insists, is a contract of 'total alienation'. Thus individuals are to vote in disregard of their private interests. What matters to each citizen — that is, to each individual *qua* indivisible part of the sovereign — can only be the interest of the body politic itself. Rousseau calls this interest general. The citizen's will is therefore the general will, the will that aims at realizing the general interest. Thus the social contract, which is 'everywhere the same', reduced to its essence, reads: 'Each of us places his person and all his power in common under the supreme direction of the general will; and as one we receive each member as an indivisible part of the whole.'[5] Through this contract, sovereignty becomes 'the exercise of the general will'.[6]

Sovereignty therefore requires nothing less than a change in individuals' dispositions which, in the state of nature as in modern civil society, are characteristically self-interested. As Hobbes had shown, private interest motivates the social contract and makes it possible. But, despite Hobbes's contrary view, private interest requires its own transformation. What individuals in a state of nature must do to achieve the sovereignty of the general will — and thereby realize essential autonomy and become the moral agents they potentially are — is forsake private for general interests. They must become pure moral personalities in the Kantian sense; integral parts of that moral and collective body which, to escape an increasingly untenable state of nature, it is their (private) interest to construct.

Sovereignty is realized, then, insofar as reason directs individuals' actions. But reason itself is transformed by the establishment of sovereignty. In the state of nature, rational agents are prudent; and prudence requires that we enter into political arrangements. But these arrangements cannot continue so long as individuals only continue to act prudently. Prudence is sensitive to what distinguishes one individual from another, to what is particular to each of us. What concerns the sovereign, however, is the general interest. Then to act rationally as a citizen, an indivisible part of the sovereign, is to act in disregard of prudence, in favour of the interests of the (political) community the social contract creates. To be moved by a general will is to assess alternatives for action and social choice with a view to realizing the interests of the state.

In identifying the interests of the state with the general interest, Rousseau assumes that political communities, constituted as states, have interests in just the way that individuals in a state of nature do. This claim is problematic, but not for its evident divergence from the facts. The claim is not that actual political communities have general interests. Rousseau would be among the first to concede that *de facto* states are seldom if ever moved by a single will. The general interest is the interest of the *de jure* state. Thus Rousseau's declaration of the existence of general interests can withstand the challenge Marxists or liberals might level by insisting that, as a matter of fact, actual states are profoundly divided and that the constituents of these communities (conceived as social classes, as pluralist groups or as individuals) have interests that are ultimately and inexorably independent or even antagonistic. So long as it is possible for *de jure* states to exist, the general will remains 'unalterable and pure', even if it never anywhere has actually existed and even if, as Rousseau seems to have believed, it likely never will. The claim that there is always a general interest is problematic in just the way the *de jure* state is. In the next chapters it will become clear that Rousseau's case for the coherence and possible applicability of the *de jure* state cannot be sustained; that given human nature and the human condition and also the constraints of historical possibility, general interests can exist only at the end of an historical trajectory that effectively undoes the conditions that, in Rousseau's view, make states necessary.

The general interest is the interest of the *de jure* state. But the general will is not the will of a supra-individual, collective entity. The general will aims at the general interest. But the general interest is the 'true' interest of each individual. The general interest, in other words, is what each individual would will were reason in control. It is always an individual's will; a will that aims at an individual's interests as a rational being. In this sense, the general interest *is* the interest of the community: not because the community is an entity with a will of its own, but because, in Rousseau's construction, the community's interest *is* each individual's true interest. Reason requires the creation of an association of individuals moved by a single will or, what comes to the same thing, the subordination of private wills to the general will.

Reason, including the reason that guides self-interested individuals in the state of nature, does not individuate. Interests individuate. Thus it is not in virtue of different rationalities that individuals act disjointedly and even antagonistically, but because they will disjointed and antagonistic ends. The social contract dissolves these differences. When as citizens we assess what is to be done, what distinguishes us as individuals matters only insofar as it bears on the general interest; an interest that, in Rousseau's account, is emphatically not an aggregation of the private interests of the individuals who comprise the political community. As a citizen, my private interest has no special bearing even on my own deliberations. Indeed, private interests have no bearing at all on what is to be done. I am to treat others as others would treat me; and to treat myself as I would treat others — as an indivisible part of the whole community formed by the social contract. The citizen judges from the standpoint of generality; according to the standard Kant expressed in the categorical imperative. We choose for ourselves, but in our capacity as components of a whole in which individuality is realized as pure (that is, empirically undifferentiated) moral personality, not particular (empirical) difference.

What the general will is with respect to particular issues will depend on circumstances in just the way that private interests do. At this level of abstraction, Rousseau cannot specify the material object of the will, the general interest, but only assert its existence. In this regard, there is an evident parallel with the Kantian view of moral law which is also specified formally through the device of generality and also asserted as a condition for the possibility of rights and duties.[7] There is indeed a conceptual affinity at an even more fundamental level. For both Rousseau and Kant, the dimension of human existence where rights and duties exist, the moral order, depends on a view of freedom as obedience to laws of one's own making insofar as reason governs, that is, on autonomy in the very special sense Kant, following Rousseau, elaborated.

The Paradox of Sovereignty

All states, actual or ideal, coordinate individuals' behaviour. It has become commonplace to say that states achieve this result by the use or threat of force; that states are essentially monopolistic organizations of 'legitimate violence'.[8] On this point, Hobbes was emphatic, as were Bodin and Macchiavelli before him and Marx and Weber, among many others, after. Rousseau does not disagree. The *de jure* state commands legitimately. But like states — actual or imagined — that command illegitimately, it enforces its commands coercively. Rousseau's state is a condition for the possibility of human beings fulfilling their destinies as moral beings. This view of what the state ideally does is original and, retrospectively, profound. But in conceiving how the state achieves this end, Rousseau's understanding accords with the dominant view.

In effect, Rousseau endorsed Hobbes's argument for the necessity of states.[9] Like Hobbes, he recast Augustine's account of coordination through force in secular form, showing how that aspect of human psychology that makes coordination necessary also makes it possible. In Augustine's scheme, Sin — conceived as love for the things of this world — threatens to undo even that very minimal level of civil peace required for the execution of God's providential design. But Sin can be met in kind. If it is love of the things of this world that incites disorder, then fear of losing these worldly things makes sanctions possible; and through sanctions behaviour can be controlled. For Hobbes, private interest (to use Rousseau's expression) plays a role analogous to Sin, rendering us like Fallen Man: acquisitive, competitive, diffident and anxious. Thus private interest threatens continually to disrupt order to the detriment of our (private) interests. In Rousseau's view, this Hobbesian concern pales before the threat private interest poses to autonomy and therefore to the realization of essential humanity. But despite this difference, Hobbes's rationale stands: private interest makes sanctions necessary and possible. We can coerce others by appealing to their (private) interests, by threatening them with the loss of what they value. In this way, we can contrive a coercive force capable of controlling such beings as we are, escape the state of nature and, Rousseau would add, realize the autonomy that is the condition for a fully human life.

There is no way to impose this force from outside. 'Men,' Rousseau insisted, 'cannot engender new forces, but merely unite and direct existing ones.'[10] The task is to construct, from what we already have at hand, a force that is external to each of our forces; an apparatus, to use Marx's metaphor, instrumental for the repression of behaviour inimical to civil peace and the realization of the general will. That apparatus is created through the establishment by contract of a sovereign sufficiently powerful — in consequence of 'the total alienation by each associate of all his rights' — to compel compliance by enforcing sanctions. In this way, individuals end the state of war by altering the structure of benefits and burdens they severally confront, through a redeployment of the forces at their disposition.

Hobbes's sovereign achieves this result unproblematically. Authorized by each party to the social contract to represent the authorizing party in matters of social control, the sovereign is literally external to the contract. He is not himself a contracting party and is not, therefore, bound by any agreements, including even the social contract itself. Thus individuals make the sovereign their master and, in Rousseau's terms, become his 'slaves'.[11] But this 'solution' contradicts the principal condition for a legitmate contract in Rousseau's formulation: it violates autonomy. In contrast, autonomy *is* maintained in the account Rousseau provided. Rousseau's sovereign is the people themselves in a new 'form of association', and the sovereign's will is the will of each person insofar as reason is in control. In obeying the sovereign, people therefore obey only themselves. Autonomy is realized; and there is no question of 'slavery'. It therefore seems that we can have authority and autonomy together; we need only become masters over ourselves. This is why Rousseau insisted that there is only a difference in 'aspect' between rulers and ruled; between citizens and subjects or, collectively, between the sovereign and the state.[12]

But how, then, is behaviour to be coordinated externally? If Rousseau could fault Hobbes for achieving authority without autonomy, surely Rousseau is vulnerable to the charge of achieving autonomy without authority or, more precisely, without political authority — authority operating upon, rather than within, individuals. In short, the condition for legitimating a force to coordinate individuals' behaviour precludes the possibility of constituting a force capable of doing so. There is either force or authority but not both together. Yet, Rousseau did conceive both together; the community the social contract establishes both is and is not essentially coercive. Moreover, this paradox is insurmountable so long as Kantian values are joined to a Hobbesian conception of 'the fundamental problem of political life'. After Hobbes, the state must be coercive if it is to end the state of nature. But, despite Hobbes, it cannot be coercive if the state of nature is to be replaced.

This paradox is symptomatic of the limitations of Kantianism as a framework for thinking philosophically about the state. But Rousseau's Kantianism is hardly unalloyed and his paradoxes are generally fruitful. It is, in this case, the paradoxical character of sovereignty in Rousseau's thought that allows the non-Kantian component of his political philosophy to coexist with Kantianism in what appears to be a system. This 'system' yields insights into the nature of the state and its future. It is therefore well temporarily to accept what Rousseau says about sovereignty at its word; and to examine what it permits him to go on to do.

Why States?

To this end, it is worth continuing the account Rousseau developed in the opening pages of *The Social Contract* in order to pursue his case for the necessity of states. We already know why states are necessary for individuals in a state of nature. Nothing else will insure civil order and realize essential autonomy. But why, once established, are states necessary in perpetuity? It would seem, after Marx, that a way out of the paradox of sovereignty might be to historicize Rousseau's story: to see the state as an episode on the way to an internally co-ordinated association of persons, a ladder for climbing out of the state of nature into the republic of ends. Rousseau resisted this move. Plainly and unabashedly, he conceived sovereignty ahistorically. This stance was not adopted for want of an alternative, even if, as is commonly supposed, 'a sense of history' was foreign to his milieu. Rousseau plainly was aware of the relevance of history for politics, as we shall go on to see. His ahistoricism on the question of sovereignty was more principled than inadvertent.

By construing the *de jure* state as an eternal and immutable ideal, Rousseau precluded any 'historical' resolution to the paradox of sovereignty. However he did advance a view of the human condition and of human limitations that redounds throughout his reflections on politics, entering even into his 'deduction' of the idea of the state. For Rousseau, as for Kant, human nature resists putting reason in control.[13] We humans are, of course, capable of rational self-determination. But we are susceptible as well to irrational determinations, to acting from inclination and, at least where private property structures social interactions, from calculations of self-interest.[14] Even in *de jure* states, we will be moved both by reason and by passion; and since passion, for Rousseau as for Kant, is always non-rational and often irrational, we are forever pulled both towards and away from the moral order sovereignty makes possible. Moral recalcitrance arising out of the inexorability of passion is a stubborn fact with which even an ahistorical investigation of sovereignty must contend. That Rousseau conceived the 'end' of human association as a state therefore appears to be a concession to this aspect of the human condition, to the all-too-human obstacles we inevitably raise for ourselves in the way of full rational self-determination.

In Rousseau's view, a coercive apparatus will therefore always be with us, though within the parameters imposed by human nature, it can be progressively diminished. This, in fact, was the point of most of the practical political measures Rousseau proposed. Rousseau's politics are a protracted struggle to *educate* humanity towards citizenship; to foster rationality and suppress irrationality. But the possibilities for change are finally limited. Passion cannot be entirely overcome, even if it can be largely suppressed or rendered benign. Therefore a coercive apparatus is unavoidable. Some of the people all of the time and all of the people some of the time will need to be 'forced to be free'.

We might therefore conclude that states, in Rousseau's view, are second-best approximations of internally coordinated communities, necessitated by the inexorable recalcitrance of human nature. At the limit, where reason is fully in control, states would wither away for want of a sufficient reason. But this conclusion, though suggestive and even prescient, is misleading. What it shows is only that violence is likely to remain a feature of organized human communities; that human nature is reformable, but never to the point where coercive public force can pass away entirely. The withering away of public coercive violence is therefore not an historical destination, in Rousseau's view, but an ahistorical implication of his theory of sovereignty. This implication cannot be realized historically so long as human beings remain recalcitrant to reason, so long as their wills never quite become what Kant deemed 'holy'.

However the existence of a state apparatus — that is, of means for exercising legitimate violence — is only superficially the issue; or rather it is the issue only insofar as we respect the paradoxical structure of Rousseau's 'system'. What matters, once the distinct strains of the system are disaggregated, is the purpose this apparatus serves. For Rousseau as for Hobbes, public coercive force ends the state of nature by forging a community based on a single will, the will of the sovereign. Yet since Rousseau's sovereign is the people themselves united by a general will, force, insofar as it still has a use, can only serve the autonomy of each associate by supporting the exercise of the general will. The state apparatus may not quite wither away, but the state, conceived as an association of persons grounded in force, would cease to be. A community organized through the fear of sanctions would pass into an association of autonomous persons coordinated through the compulsion of reason.

The *De Jure* State

That Rousseau seems to have provided an account of political right and even, as he claimed, of sovereignty is a consequence of a systematic equivocation. The *de jure* state does coordinate behaviour coercively. But it is not *essentially* coercive. In adopting Hobbes's account of the rationale for states, Rousseau appears to conclude differently. Like Hobbes, Rousseau insisted that there be no concessions to the state of nature, no rights retained by individuals. The state of nature can only be ended, he insisted, with individuals' 'forces' alienated totally to the sovereign. In this sense, the state *is* grounded in force: the collective forces of its individual constitutents. But the burden of Rousseau's argument is to show that 'total alienation by each associate of all his rights' is rationally required; that the grounding of the *de jure* state is the rational will of each 'associate' — that is, of each individual *qua* citizen. Might does not make right,[15] as it does for Hobbes, but only backs right by supporting the claims of reason. The 'moral and collective body' the social contract founds can be expected to use force against the irrationally recalcitrant. If it does so, it is not because it is essentially violent, but because it is rational.

The paradox of sovereignty cannot be resolved by somehow combining authority and autonomy together. But it can be dissipated by adhering rigorously to one or the other of Rousseau's two concepts of the state. In view of the importance Rousseau attached to autonomy, it is clear which concept should be retained. In the final analysis, the *de jure* state is based on reason. It is not just a second-best approximation of the republic of ends, but the republic of ends itself.

This state, when it uses force, coerces its associates in the way individuals might alter the physical environments they confront in order better to constrain their future behaviour and thereby execute their respective private wills. In both cases, force is part of an indirect strategy for bringing about what reason requires in circumstances where a more direct effort is unfeasible.[16] Self-constraint is an individual analogue to public, coercive force; particularly if, like Rousseau, we suppose that the whole community, like an individual, is moved by a single will. Then the *de jure* state only superficially resembles the states envisaged by other political philosophers. Their states are essentially violent; Rousseau's is violent only 'accidentally', in consequence of human limitations independent of the case for sovereignty. As much as in the state of nature, sovereignty in Rousseau's state lies within. Where the paradox of sovereignty is resolved in favour of autonomy over authority, there is no external force coordinating behaviour coercively but only the people themselves contriving to overcome a collective weakness of will.

If human beings are indeed as recalcitrant as Rousseau sometimes supposed, the state might frequently take recourse to force, just as a weak-willed individual might frequently utilize physical constraints strategically. It would be natural, then, to conflate an essentially rational entity that uses violence frequently with an entity that is essentially violent. Appearances, or rather speculations about appearances, would be deceptive. Wittingly or not, Rousseau traded on this deception; identifying an internalized 'harmony of rational wills,' that uses violence as an indirect strategy for keeping its 'indivisible' component parts in line, with an external force that compels compliance through the use or threat of force. But, again, this is a constructive equivocation. For it leads Rousseau, despite his Kantianism, to depict what the social contract founds as a state; and then to join his reflections on this state and its politics — reflections that implicitly raise the question of the possibility of anarchy — with a non-Kantian sensitivity to the historicity and specificity of politics.

2
Rousseau's Politics

Rousseau's theory of sovereignty is joined with the rest of his reflections on politics with at least the appearance of a system; his Kantianism does motivate a political system — at least apparently. Thus the guiding principle underlying the various measures Rousseau proposed for the *de jure* state is to make actual what sovereignty requires: the governance of reason over passion or, what comes to the same thing, the supremacy of the general will over private wills. We have seen how this objective, if realized, implies the end of the state (in the traditional sense) for want of a sufficient reason for its continuance. Where reason governs, the state gives way to a republic of ends. But, in consequence of what Rousseau took to be timeless human limitations, he did not depict the republic of ends as an historical destination. It is, instead, the extreme realization of one side of human experience: towards which, at best, institutions and practices may tend. Sovereignty, paradoxically, is a goal of legitimate institutions at the same time that it is a condition for their legitimacy.

The Kantian component of Rousseau's thought is ahistorical and pessimistic. Where this strain dominates, we are led to envisage the end of the state more as a regulative idea than as a political objective. However, Kantian ahistoricism and pessimism are excisable from the recommendations Rousseau proposed for approaching this ever elusive ideal. Rousseau's importance for political philosophy is as much evident in these practical political recommendations as in the Kantian vision he 'discovered'. Despite their anachronistic and utopian aspects, these measures or the principles that motivate them, are pertinent too for socialist political theory and for joining Rousseauean political philosophy with aspects of Marxian thought.

As a Kantian, Rousseau conceived the measures he proposed as moves in an eternally human drama where reason and passion contend for dominance over individuals' will. Politics, then, is a struggle for the soul of Everyman, not a battle played out in history under ever-changing constraints for ever-changing stakes. This ahistorical view of politics accords with the ahistoricism and pessimism that underlies Rousseau's account of sovereignty. But it is also at considerable remove from any conceivable politics 'taking men as they are'. However much he may have struggled to present a politics consistent with his theory of sovereignty, Rousseau saw more clearly than his predecessors and the vast majority of his successors too that in our world political struggles are always essentially localized in time and place. In that eternal and unchanging Platonic heaven where the idea of the state resides, politics, finally, has no niche.

Thus Rousseau also conceived the measures he proposed as specific and conjunctural; proper not 'under the aspect of eternity' but in historically determinate conditions. Rousseau's special contribution, I will argue, consists not just in calling attention to the specificity of politics and casting insight on particular political matters but in anticipating a theory of the specificity of politics. Some elements of that theory, left in a rudimentary state by Rousseau, were later developed significantly by Rousseau's disciples and critics, and also by Marx and his successors. But Marxians, to their detriment, have failed to develop or even to acknowledge other important Rousseauean contributions. Arguably also, Rousseau too failed to recognize all the riches he had discovered, absorbed as he was in the vain project of reflecting on politics in the wake of his discovery of the moral universe Kant would subsequently explore.

Thus in Rousseau's texts, politics is conceived ahistorically; but politics is discussed as if it were essentially historical. The assumption that human beings are capable of full rational self-determination allowed Rousseau to 'deduce' the concept of sovereignty. But his recognition of the irreducible specificity of politics, in plain opposition to the Kantian strain of his thought, allowed Rousseau to contribute enormously to the understanding of actual politics. In virtue of this inconsistency, Rousseau provided elements of a theory of political feasibility, the fundamental concern for any political philosophy that would be, at once, both visionary and non-utopian.

It will be convenient to distinguish Rousseau's political economic recommendations from the other measures he proposed. Marx would, of course, later make this division itself a matter of theory. Considering Rousseauean politics in terms of this categorial division will help give Rousseau's political speculations structure, and also help eventually in fusing Rousseauean thought with substantive Marxian positions.

Political Economy

If, in thinking about sovereignty, Rousseau directly anticipated substantive Kantian positions, in thinking about political economy, he presciently, though anachronistically, anticipated some fundamental Marxian views. Rousseau does not have much to say about political economy *per se.* There are only oblique declarations in *The Social Contract* and casual discussions scattered among his recommendations for existing political communities.[1] Still, if only from remarks made in passing, there is the plain suggestion that, in Marx's metaphor, political superstructures rest upon appropriate economic bases. Rousseau even suggested in *The Social Contract* that the *de jure* state supposes a particular form of economic organization similar in one crucial respect to communism. But the economic order Rousseau imagined is not communist or even socialist. Nor is it a feasible form of capitalism. Rousseau's economic prescriptions, taken at their word, are nostalgic and impracticable, the stuff of 'reverie', not practical politics. Rousseau was not an innovator in economic theory. His economic proposals draw on received, eighteenth-century understandings to which Rousseau accorded the 'obviousness' of common sense. The economic common sense of Rousseau's day, however, seems nonsense two centuries later. His economic recommendations are therefore of little interest in themselves. It is the rationale that motivates them that warrants reflection.

The *de jure* state superintends a society of small independent producers — of yeoman farmers and urban artisans — each owning the means of production with which they labour, and each exchanging the products of labour that are not directly consumed in free markets.[2] What Rousseau envisaged is, in effect, Adam Smith's 'early and rude state of society': a pre-industrial economic order with private ownership of means of production and little division of labour, and without significant differences in the distribution of income or wealth. Since productive resources are privately owned, the economic order of the *de jure* state is capitalist.[3] But unlike historical capitalisms, this capitalism is egalitarian and, like communism, classless. Rousseau's intended or inadvertent disregard of relations within households (between husbands and wives and between fathers and children) apart, everyone has approximately the same resources, and everyone stands in the same proprietary relation to society's means of production.

However, to describe the *de jure* state as classless is anachronistic. Strictly speaking, Rousseau had no notion of class in the Marxian sense, but only of differences in wealth and rank. What Rousseau wanted to avoid was not exactly the division of society into masters and slaves, lords and serfs, capitalists and proletarians, but into rich and poor. Thus he enjoined the citizens of the *de jure* state 'to tolerate neither rich people nor beggars'. For where these estates exist, commerce in freedom is inevitable. 'These two conditions, naturally inseparable, are equally fatal to the general welfare; from the one class spring tyrants, from the other, the supporters of tyranny; it is always between these that the traffic in public liberty is carried on; the one buys and the other sells.'[4]

There is, however, a more fundamental danger posed by the division of society into rich and poor that is a special case of the menace Rousseau thought all social groups, whatever their bases, pose: the danger that the common interests of individuals in these groups — private interests, in Rousseau's scheme, because they are not interests of the community as such — will undermine the exercise of the general will. This danger becomes particularly menacing if we imagine society divided into classes in Marx's sense. Class divisions represent fundamental social cleavages inimical to any putative consensus on ends. In class-divided societies, the general will is systematically eluded. To maintain the sovereignty of the general will, Rousseau asserted a direct, unmediated relation between individuals and 'the whole community'. Marxian classes, however, are among the most profound mediations conceivable. Rousseau, again, did not quite acknowledge Marxian class divisions. In insisting that all economic agents stand in the same relations to society's means of production, though, he effectively, if unwittingly, promoted the view that legitimate political institutions presuppose classlessness.

To prevent the division of society into (non-Marxian) 'classes' or, better, 'estates' of rich and poor, Rousseau insisted that in the *de jure* state 'no citizen should be rich enough to be able to buy another, and none poor enough to be forced to sell himself.'[5] But he did not explain how this condition might be achieved; nor did he discuss the role of the state in its implementation. These omissions are serious: where resources are privately owned and markets organize trade, some individuals will eventually come to hold vast resources and others none at all. Tendentially, society will be divided into capitalists, who own all there is to own, and proletarians, who own nothing. Rousseau was aware of this problem and proposed measures for addressing it. But he provided no specifically economic remedies. In a word, Rousseau's economic prescriptions are self-defeating: the system he endorsed, if left to develop according to its proper 'laws of motion', would in short order undo itself. What is pertinent in Rousseau's vision, then, are the intuitions that motivate it: his sense of the importance of equality, and his determination not to allow the formation of relatively fixed coalitions with common interests distinct from the general interest. In its actual specifications, Rousseau's vision is fantasy.

Before turning to the remedies Rousseau proposed to counteract the self-defeating tendency of the system he endorsed, it will be instructive to try to account for his endorsement of this system. Since he nowhere defended yeoman capitalism directly, we can only impute a rationale. Still, the outlines of a case are evident enough. Like his contemporaries, Rousseau was shortsighted in imagining alternatives. Shortsightedness, however, is not the whole story. Nor is the story completed by familiar claims that are invoked, even today, in support of (capitalist) markets: that market arrangements maximize individuals' freedom to do as they please with their possessions; or augment welfare by permitting mutually advantageous trades; or advance justice by proscribing unfair limitations on what individuals can do with what they own.[6]

Rousseau was little concerned with 'natural liberty', the unrestrained freedom of the state of nature, or welfare or even justice. What motivated Rousseau's vision of a society of small, independent, property-owning producers was, instead, the support this system seems to lend to freedom in the sense that mattered for him: freedom as *autonomy* or rational self-determination.

In this regard, the classlessness of simple yeoman society is of paramount importance. Of all the alternatives eighteenth-century political economists conceived, the economic system Rousseau endorsed is the one most likely to further the autonomy of notionally equal citizens because it alone consigns no one to an economically subordinate class, but instead treats individuals equally, eliminating all institutional advantages and disadvantages. However, classlessness, though necessary, is not sufficient for autonomy. In intimating what would be sufficient, Rousseau, again, 'discovered' more than he knew. Inadvertently and in disregard of the ahistoricism manifest in his account of sovereignty and political obligation, Rousseau discovered the role abundance must play in the attempt to establish a community of autonomous agents, a republic of ends, on earth.

Insofar as a considered view can be teased out of sparse and scattered indications, Rousseau seems to have believed that yeoman capitalism is preferable to any alternative economic order because it leaves individuals equally and well provided with the means for life. One recalls that, in Rousseau's account, the civil society that underlies the *de jure* state is constituted by market transactions of small, independent producers, each owning the means of production with which they labour and each relatively self-sufficient. It is self-sufficiency that advances autonomy. Because producers are self-sufficient, they are not compelled by circumstances to trade, but do so instead from freely formed desires — from a propensity, as Adam Smith wrote in *The Wealth of Nations*, 'to truck, barter and exchange'. Market transactions, then, will typically be exchanges of unwanted surplus, not of necessities. And since, in contrast to historically possible capitalisms, producers own the means of production with which they labour, everyone has the means to set their own labour to work. There is, therefore, no structural incentive to sell either labour or the products of labour. With regard to terms of trade, all parties are equal. Exchanges, then, are not only voluntary but fully free in the sense Rousseau intended: they are autonomously determined, motivated by ends individuals set before themselves.

Needless to say, self-sufficiency is an unlikely — indeed, utopian — expectation; incompatible with a division of labour, the existence of towns, of commerce and industry, and even with the contingencies of nature in any world remotely like our own. 'Taking men as they are', we cannot expect general self-sufficiency. We therefore cannot realistically expect to advance autonomy through the economic measures Rousseau recommended. These recommendations are instructive nevertheless. Without quite being aware, Rousseau effectively demonstrated the importance — for autonomy's sake — of overcoming class divisions in conditions of abundance. Where he erred was in attempting to implement these conditions in a self-defeating way and in an historically impossible form.

Rousseau's political writings are hardly bereft of proposals for mitigating at least the self-defeating tendencies of the system he advocated. Later chapters will attempt to correct Rousseau's economic prescriptions by appealing first indirectly, then expressly to Marxian positions on historical possibility. In the remainder of this chapter, by reflecting on Rousseau's attempts to counter the tendency of his favoured economic order to undo itself, we will gain an initial purchase on the correction to the correction — the indispensable support Rousseauean political theory provides for the Marxian project.

Ideological Interventions

Rousseau was aware of the difficulty of maintaining a simple, yeoman society of property owners in the face of the tendency of markets, even among initially self-sufficient traders, to foster capital accumulation and its concomitant, proletarianization. He proposed that the *de jure* state combat this tendency of its economic base ideologically, as we would say nowadays — through measures aimed at transforming *moeurs*, 'manners and morals'. What guided his political recommendations was a determination to direct what Rousseau's contemporaries called 'opinion' and, in doing so, to change persons from rational egoists, intent on accumulating resources and dominating others, to citizens, moved by republican virtue and a taste for the simplicity and order of yeoman life. Only the spirit of citizenship, Rousseau thought, can countervail the tendency for wealth to accumulate beyond acceptable limits. Rousseauean civil society is sustainable if and only if individuals are citizens before they are capitalists.

This consideration, though important in its own right, is only one instance of Rousseau's overriding conviction that the spirit of citizenship is essential for making the exercise of the general will actual by eliminating private interest from public life. Thus opinion becomes the principal site of struggle in all of Rousseau's political reflections: for sustaining the economic base of the *de jure* state but also, more generally, in the contest waged inside each individual between the private and the general will.

Rousseau insisted, therefore, that state institutions be constructed with a view to forming citizens. All social practices — the establishment of public spectacles and sporting events, the organization of the educational system, the establishment of civil religion, and even the government itself — are to be arranged with this end in view.[7] Whatever encourages individual differences and competition or promotes a sense of group (as opposed to state) identification is to be suppressed. Whatever fosters a sense of social solidarity and dedication to public endeavours or promotes virtue, simplicity and the abhorrence of luxury is to be encouraged. A generalized disposition to act in ways appropriate for citizens is the precondition for legitimacy. The political task, therefore, is to make this precondition actual. Sovereignty requires individuals educated to the generality of the will.

This orientation carries over even into Rousseau's recommendations for existing political communities in Poland and Corsica.[8] Apparently, Rousseau believed that historical circumstance and the inexorability of recalcitrant passion made the *de jure* state of *The Social Contract* impracticable, even in those areas of Europe least corrupted by deleterious 'civilization'. He therefore turned, as a moral theorist, to what is realizable in oneself regardless of the political circumstances with which one must contend and, as a political theorist, to contriving second-best approximations to the ideal theory of *The Social Contract*.[9] The dispositions he sought to inculcate, even in the face of an overwhelming pessimism, however, remain constant. Throughout his political writings, Rousseau advocated capitalist social relations, but profoundly non-capitalist *moeurs*.

The particular measures Rousseau proposed, whether for the ideal state of *The Social Contract* or for *de facto* states, are never simply ahistorical technical manipulations, contrived to bring about particular effects regardless of circumstances. Even if, in consequence of his Kantianism, Rousseau tends to view politics as an ahistorical struggle between reason and passion, the measures he proposed for waging this struggle are always utterly and irreducibly conjunctural. It is contingent happenstance — the nature of the population, its traditions and history, its circumstances and conditions — that determines what is or is not instrumental for promoting virtuous dispositions and therefore, ultimately, the generality of the will. The social contract itself is 'everywhere and always the same'. Yet the means by which it may be realized or, more realistically, approximated are as varied as the peoples and circumstances that populate the globe.

Nowhere is the conjunctural character of politics more evident than in the extended discussion in Book 3 of *The Social Contract* of forms of government.[10] Government is that institutional apparatus established by the sovereign people, from which it derives its authority, for the purpose of executing the sovereign's enactments. It is, as it were, 'the executive committee' of the state. The *de jure* state must, of course, have a government, but there is no particular form of government it must have. Indeed, Rousseau is adamant that, for a given territory or population, there is no mechanical procedure for determining what the best form of government is. There are only general guidelines that can be provided, as Rousseau attempted throughout Book 3. But in the end, the determination of the best form of government remains indeterminate at the level of abstraction at which *The Social Contract* is posed. What is best for a particular territory or population is, literally, particular to that territory or population. Circumstance and tradition matter far more than philosophical speculation or derivation from the 'first principles' of political association.

Thus in determining forms of government and other fundamental institutional practices of the *de jure* state, Rousseau accorded considerable weight to the art of the 'lawgiver',[11] that charismatic figure like Moses or Solon, who intervenes early in the lives of states to guide the construction of basic constitutional forms and to help establish the principal features of a community's political culture. A state will succeed if it has the good fortune to have a wise and persuasive lawgiver, capable of forming the political community without usurping the sovereign power that, we know, can only reside with the people themselves. Ultimately, then, the fate of actual states is beyond the power of philosophy to direct or even conceive. The lawgiver's work is an art, informed by wisdom not science. What Pascal called *l'esprit de geometrie* is appropriately deployed in founding the state. In forming and directing the state, at its inception particularly but also throughout its life, what is required is *l'esprit de finesse*.

This non- or extra-Kantian sensitivity to the particularity of politics is, however, joined with a notion of the *objective* of politics, shaped in large part by Rousseau's Kantian concerns. It is not for its own sake that Rousseau prescribes finesse in political affairs. What ought to guide deliberations over institutional arrangements and inform our judgements of actual or proposed political measures is their effects. What matters, in other words, is not the measures themselves, but their consequences for promoting or impeding education towards citizenship, towards *moeurs* conducive to the supremacy of the general will. Thus Rousseau's proposals are debatable even in the circumstances he envisaged. It is far from clear, for example, that the simple, yeoman society Rousseau prescribed would have appeared viable even to his contemporaries in the face of the emerging capitalist organization of late eighteenth-century Europe. Nor are Rousseau's specifically ideological interventions — the 'golden lie' of civil religion, censorship, and other proposals for the regimentation of public life — indisputably the most efficacious means for achieving social solidarity and civic virtue. Many of these measures seem unattractive today and must have seemed so too even in Rousseau's time. They could well be challenged on Rousseauean grounds. What matters, however, is not the proposals themselves but the principle that warrants their introduction and defence. Political measures are considered and assessed according to their consequences in specific conjunctures — upon the state's 'economic base' and upon 'opinion', the human foundation of the state.

In sum, Rousseau conceived politics as an essentially historical endeavour undertaken in an essentially ahistorical struggle of wills. There is no blatant inconsistency in this view. But there is a plain tension: an implicit affirmation, framed in an express denial, of the historicity of politics.

* * *

We therefore find in Rousseau a tension with the Kantianism that shapes his view of sovereignty, a different conception of the place of politics in human life: not as the manifestation of an eternal struggle between timeless and immutable aspects of human nature, but as a contest in which the stakes can be radically different, historical outcomes. It is this non-Kantian view of politics that permits a conception of the end of the state as an historical destination, realizable in principle in consequence of its increasing superfluity. Kantianism led Rousseau to 'discover' this idea but also to derogate it as utopian. There is, however, a deep irony in this reproach. Rousseau's economic prescriptions are literally utopian: they cannot be realized in any feasible, historical society. But in failing to conceive the end of the state as a political goal, Rousseau may be conceding too much to pessimism. He may be, as it were, insufficiently visionary.

However it is premature, at this point, to draw conclusions about the end of the state. We first need an account of what is attainable in real historical time. Some of Rousseau's immediate successors — revolutionary Jacobins and conservative critics of the French Revolution — effectively identified this need and began to elaborate elements of a theory. Their reflections provide insight into what actually is utopian and what can be placed on the historical agenda.

3
Rousseau and Revolution

The extent of Rousseau's influence on the French Revolution has long been a subject of continuing debate. Since what follows depends more on self-representations and perceived connections than on actual influences, this debate will not be joined here. However, if only to supply a cautionary perspective, it is well to begin by acknowledging the controversy.

A major influence has long been claimed. Thus Edmund Burke declared: 'Who ever dreamt of Voltaire and Rousseau as legislators?' and added of *The Social Contract*, 'little did I conceive, that it could ever make revolutions, and give law to nations. But so it has'. A similar view was expressed more colourfully by Henrich Heine:

> 'Mark this, ye proud men of action; ye are nothing but unconscious hoodmen of the men of thought who, often in humblest stillness, have appointed you your inevitable task. Maximilien Robespierre was merely the hand of Jean-Jacques Rousseau, the bloody hand that drew from the womb of time the body whose soul Rousseau had created.'[2]

Many 'proud men of action' have agreed. Napoleon himself declared: 'had there been no Rousseau, there would have been no Revolution. If there had been no Revolution, I would have been impossible.'[3]

For nearly a century after Heine, this view prevailed. In more recent years, Albert Camus,[4] Hannah Arendt,[5] J.L. Talmon,[6] and Bronowski and Mazlish,[7] among others, have reiterated the traditional position. Since the 1930s, however, a number of historians have undertaken to reassess the pre-Revolutionary influence of Rousseau's political philosophy. The traditional orthodoxy, according to which Rousseau 'inspired' the French Revolution, has come to be largely supplanted, in specialized though not in popular thought, by a new orthodoxy that sees Rousseau as a moralist with little influence prior to 1789. Pioneered by the French historian Daniel Mornet,[8] and elaborated in Joan McDonald's *Rousseau and the French Revolution*,[9] the revised view maintains that Rousseau's influence has been grossly exaggerated and was in fact quite minimal. Recent scholarship has again swung back in favour of the traditional position.

But even if Rousseau's influence on the French Revolution has been exaggerated, his influence on particular revolutionaries, above all, on Robespierre is incontestable.[10] It is this influence and not the broader claim that Rousseau somehow inspired the French Revolution that is supposed in what follows.

Indeed, what I will argue here does not even depend on a strong Rousseauean influence on Robespierre. I will hold that Robespierre showed that Rousseau's political philosophy misrepresents the character of politics in the course of revolutionary change; and that Rousseau's political proposals, taken at their word, are inadequate for the tasks the French Revolution posed. That there is a clear identification on the part of Robespierre and his co-thinkers with the political theory of *The Social Contract* is, I think, beyond dispute. Then the Jacobins were unwitting critics of Rousseau, implicitly putting in question what they themselves believed. Even if their connection with Rousseau is less pronounced than I shall suppose, it would follow only that the Jacobins were critics of a position towards which they were generally indifferent. In either case, the point remains.

Whatever their quarrel with Rousseauean political theory, the Jacobins were by no means anti-Rousseauean. The critique implicit in their practice and in the speeches of Robespierre builds upon Rousseau's foundations. Theirs was, as might nowadays be said, an immanent critique. Implicitly and programmatically, Robespierre and his co-thinkers suggested corrections for the shortcomings they identified in order better to implement ideals they and Rousseau shared.

Virtue and Terror

On 5 Nivose of the Year II (Christmas Day, 1793), addressing the National Assembly on behalf of the Committee of Public Safety, Robespierre declared: 'The theory of revolutionary government is as new as the revolution that has brought it about. It should not be sought in the books of political writers, who have not foreseen this revolution, nor in the laws of tyrants who, content to abuse their power, are little concerned to investigate its legitimacy.'[11] To Robespierre's followers and perhaps also, in more contemplative moments, to Robespierre himself, this declaration must have been understood as rhetorical exaggeration. For however the Jacobins may have conceived the relation between the revolutionary government they had established and 'the laws of tyrants', Robespierre and his fellow revolutionaries certainly conceived themselves as continuing in the tradition of English and French republicanism, if not as plain disciples of Rousseau. But even if the express intent of Robespierre and other Jacobin leaders were only to put *The Social Contract* into practice (if necessary by despotic means), it still seems right, in this instance, to take Robespierre at his word. The theory implicit in Jacobin practice and epitomized in Robespierre's speeches and reports is indeed new.

When Robbespierre speaks about revolutionary government, his idiom, like Rousseau's, is generically republican: 'What is the fundamental principle of democratic or popular government? It is *virtue*, and I speak of that public virtue which performed such miracles in Greece and Rome and which is destined to perform even more astonishing miracles in republican France; of that virtue which is nothing other than love of one's country and its laws.'[12]

Like the state envisaged in *The Social Contract*, the French republic is to be composed of virtuous citizens, simple in manners and morals, dedicated to advancing general, not private, interests. However, Robespierre continues:

> If the mainspring of popular government in time of peace is virtue, its mainspring in time of revolution is *virtue and terror combined*: virtue without which terror is squalidly repressive, terror without which virtue lies disarmed. Terror is nothing other than swift, severe and inflexible justice: it is therefore an emanation of virtue; and it is not so much a principle in itself as a consequence of the general principle of democracy when applied to the most urgent needs of the nation.[13]

The formulation — 'virtue and terror combined' — is paradoxical. For all republicans, including Rousseau, the terms are inimical and even contrary: virtue is the essence of republican government; terror is the essence of its opposite, despotism.[14] But for Robespierre, so far from being contraries, terror, in conditions of social revolution, is declared an 'emanation' of virtue. Revolutionary government is based on the conjunction of these opposites.

Needless to say, Robespierre's declaration is not the conclusion of a philosophical reflection. The paradoxical conjuction of virtue and terror is more a symptom of a philosophical position than a considered philosophical claim. It is an expression of Jacobin practice. I will attempt to expose what this symptom reveals by commenting on Robespierre's formulation and on his insistence that the theory of revolutionary government based on the conjuction of virtue and terror is new.

Dictatorship

In *The Social Contract*, there is a very brief account of a form of administration that appears to anticipate the revolutionary government Robespierre led.[15] When exceptional circumstances arise such that the very existence of the state is threatened then, Rousseau maintains, exceptional measures may be taken in defence of the state. Laws may be suspended and the normal executive apparatus, concocted to execute these laws, replaced by a dictatorship of one or several magistrates. Dictatorship, however, is not quite one more governmental form, among the many discussed in Book 3 of *The Social Contract*. It is a suspension of governmental forms — a temporary and desperate expedient for saving the state, to be employed only in the gravest of circumstances.

Rousseau is, surprisingly, little concerned to reconcile what he says in defence of this expedient with his claim that sovereignty can be neither alienated nor represented. Indeed, his remarks on dictatorship casually dismiss what appears to be a plain contradiction. He writes:

> If the danger is such that the formal apparatus of law is an obstacle to our security, a supreme head is named, who may silence all the laws, and suspend for a moment the sovereign authority. In such a case, the

general will is not doubtful, and it is clear that the primary intention of the people is that the state should not perish. In this way, the suspension of the legislative power does not involve its abolition; the magistrate who silences it can make it speak; he dominates it without having to represent it; he can do everything but make laws.[16]

How 'domination' differs from 'representation' is never explained; nor are we told how this putative distinction represents a real difference. Instead, Rousseau simply asserts that, in sufficiently dire circumstances, the general will enjoins the suspension of sovereignty.

However Rousseau is very concerned to ensure that dictatorship, once initiated, does not degenerate into despotism. 'In Rome,' he writes, 'the dictators held office for six months only, and the majority abdicated before the end of this term. Had the term been longer, they would perhaps have been tempted to prolong it further still, as the Decemvirs did their term of one year. The dictator had time only to provide for the necessity which led to his election; he had no time to think of other projects.' In other words, to avoid mortal danger to the (popular) sovereign, dictatorship must be of short duration. It must not be allowed time to consolidate itself or to supplant the institutions it has suspended. On no account should the dictatorship be permitted to transform itself into a new order. Its suspension of the old order is limited to one purpose only: the restoration and protection of the institutions it has temporarily superceded.

From what, though, is the existing order to be protected? Though drawn to the historical example of Rome, Rousseau could hardly have imagined the *de jure* state threatened by civil disorders of the kind that afflicted the Roman republic. Unlike ancient Rome, the *de jure* state is classless and even homogeneous. It has no slaves, no subjugated peoples, no proletariat; in short, no social groups ready to revolt. What might necessitate dictatorship must therefore come from without: emergencies brought on, say, by wars or invasions or natural calamities. In allowing for dictatorship, Rousseau acknowledged a certain inflexibility in popular sovereignty that may render the *de jure* state incapable of dealing with the vicissitudes of a sometimes unfriendly world. Dictatorship is introduced *ad hoc* to remedy this inflexibility.

In short, Rousseau conceived dictatorship, with something less than full consistency, as a supplement to his theory of sovereignty, not his theory of government. Dictatorship is introduced to provide flexibility to institutions that might otherwise prove ill-equipped to accommodate the vicissitudes of circumstance. 'A thousand cases may arise,' Rousseau notes, 'for which the legislator has not provided, and to perceive that everything cannot be forseen is a very needful kind of foresight.'[17] In a word, dictatorship is an extraordinary institution of the state. There is no place, strictly speaking, for dictatorial government in the *de jure* state. But extraordinary circumstances may warrant short-lived dictatorial suspensions of government.

Robespierre seems to have regarded what has come to be called the Terror, the period from September 1793 to July 1794, as a dictatorship in the sense Rousseau described.[18] France was at war with most of Europe, her provinces in open revolt, her economy in ruins. The Revolution itself was in mortal danger. What choice but to suspend the constitution and invest dictatorial powers in a strong government, capable of leading the Revolution through these perils? However, the Jacobin dictatorship, the Reign of Terror, was not, in the final analysis, a Rousseauean dictatorship. Neither the situation nor the response accorded with Rousseau's prescriptions. The situation was dire, to be sure; but, for Rousseau, dire situations are confronted by political communities, not generated by them. The *de jure* state is (relatively) autarkik and always stable. It defends itself, but it does not make war. It is neither expansionist nor aggresive and its internal processes promote prosperity and peace. Revolutionary France, on the other hand, waged war, at least in part, for reasons internal to its own revolutionary dynamic. Though genuinely besieged, the Revolution was by no means an innocent victim of forces arrayed against it. Neither war nor domestic dissension (and insurrection), nor even the economic crisis descended upon France from without. What threatened the French Republic in the autumn of 1793 was, in very large measure, internally generated.

If only for this reason, we should hesitate before calling the revolutionary government Robespierre led a Rousseauean dictatorship. If that government looks like what Rousseau described, it is in part because of the absence of alternative models (owing to a lack of historical precedent), in part because of the extreme character of the measures taken.[19] How could measures so unprecedented and terrifying not be extraordinary and temporary? And even if the emergencies occasioning the

Terror — arguably even justifying it — were internally generated, surely the Terror itself was, like Rousseau's dictatorship, a suspension of normal political life. But from a twentieth-century vantage point, this sense of the situation seems less sure. The French Revolution, it now appears, altered normal politics: inaugurating a new phase in the period of revolution and counter-revolution that, since the seventeenth century, has shaped the history first of Europe and then of the entire world. Marx attempted a theoretical grounding for this change of perspective, as we shall go on to see. But even in the absence of a theory, it should seem clear to our contemporaries, if not to the French revolutionaries themselves, that what revolutionary France set in motion, though unprecedented, is unique only in the degree of its severity. The Jacobin dictatorship was a form of government, of revolutionary government, not a suspension of government. And if the Terror, in its bloody excesses, occasioned what is exceptional and temporary, revolutionary government itself, we now can see, need not be either.

The leaders of the Terror, including Robespierre, always insisted that with the end of the war and a diminution of internal and economic troubles, there would be a return to the 1793 Constitution. In fact, the Terror was not ended voluntarily but by violent overthrow on 9 Thermidor of the Year II (July 1794). It is vain to speculate what would otherwise have happened. This much is clear: a revolutionary dynamic had been set in motion that could advance or retreat but no longer be set aside. To resume the *status quo ante* after a temporary suspension was out of the question. Whatever their prior expectations, the French revolutionaries came to realize in practice, if not quite in theory, a lesson that has yet to be fully appreciated: that social revolution is not a *moment* of transition, an event of brief duration and fixed scope, but a period of internal transformation, fraught with unforeseeable vicissitudes, lasting for an indefinite duration, and that in this process of uncertain outcome the role of government is crucial.

The Jacobins discovered (without quite knowing they had) that the protection and propogation of revolution, if need be by supra-legal means, is a constant exigency, not a temporary and exceptional expedient; and that this task requires a state that advances certain interests over others. They discovered, in other words, that in revolutionary times the general will cannot be exercised if, indeed, it makes sense to speak of a general will at all. It is therefore mistaken to regard any government as an 'executor' of the sovereign's will or to construe dictatorship as a temporary suspension of sovereignty in order to save it. Revolutionary events collapsed Rousseau's distinction and transformed the idea of government itself.

If neither Robespierre nor any of his contemporaries quite succeeded in formulating what their practice implicitly supposed, the fault lies, to some substantial degree, with the legacy left by Rousseau. Whatever untapped resources it may provide for a theory of post-capitalist political forms, Rousseauean thought impedes the development of an adequate account of the place of politics in the process of revolutionary change. It will become evident that Marxian theory renders Robespierre's revolutionary politics comprehensible in ways Robespierre could only intimate through suggestive, but finally incoherent, paradoxical declarations.

Virtue

In the final chapter of Book 2 of *The Social Contract*, at the conclusion of a discussion on the scope and variety of laws, Rousseau declares there to be a type of law

> '... which is graven neither on marble nor on brass, but in the hearts of citizens; a law which creates the real constitution of the state, which acquires new strength daily, which when other laws grow old or pass away, revives them or supplies their place, preserves a people in the spirit of their institutions and imperceptibly substitutes the force of habit for that of authority. I speak of manners [*moeurs*], customs and above all of opinion — a part unknown to our politicans, but one on which the success of all the rest depends ...'[20]

Moeurs, custom and opinion play this role because they shape individuals' wills and, we know, a principal objective of Rousseau's politics is precisely to promote a type of will, the general will, 'which alone renders man truly master of himself'.[21] To foster the general will is tantamount to forming citizens, individuals *qua* bearers of the general will. Citizenship, then, is what is at stake in the contest of wills Rousseau envisions.

In elaborating an account of the transformative role of political institutions, Rousseau broke new ground. But the goal of the measures he proposed was hardly original. The character-type Rousseau would promote is widely celebrated among political thinkers in the republican tradition. For Rousseau as for all the rest, what is to be instilled is virtue.

Virtue, in the sense in question, is the subordination of one's own interests to the interests of one's community. Virtue, then, is an essentially social concept, fundamentally opposed to egoism in all its varieties. It is a concept proper more to the classical than the Christian roots of western political theory. Despite the evident piety of many republicians and despite the strong historical connection joining republicanism and Calvinism (evident also in Rousseau's writings), personal salvation is not the end virtue serves. To be for virtue is to suppose that human beings are essentially political animals and that political association and activity are necessary for a fully human life. Robinson Crusoe alone on his island could not be virtuous, except in society with his servant Friday. For the same reason, the path to virtue cannot lie in ascetic retreat or abandonment of the world, but in active engagement in wordly affairs and, above all, in political institutions.[22]

Rousseau took over this understanding at the same time that he supplied virtue with a special sense consonant with his account of the general will and its politics. In *The Social Contract*, virtue is tantamount to subordination of one's private to one's general will or, what comes to the same thing, to the governance of (practical) reason. Then the rational agent, the citizen and the virtuous person are one. To the extent the Jacobin call to create the Republic of Virtue is Rousseauean and not just republican in inspiration, it enjoins creating the republic *tout court*, by making the social contract — which as a Platonic idea, always exists and is everywhere the same — actual. The Republic of Virtue, then, literally is the *de jure* state.

That this was the *express* understanding of many Jacobins, and particularly of Robespierre, is suggested by the role played by equality in Robespierre's reflections on virtue. In his discourse 'On the Principles of Political Morality', after reaffirming the centrality of virtue, Robespierre asked: 'But what is virtue?' And he replied: '. . . this virtue is nothing other than the love of one's country and its laws. But as the meaning (*sens*) of the republic or of democracy is equality, it follows that love of country necessarily includes love of equality.' And he declares further on: 'Since the soul of the republic is virtue and equality, and since our end is to establish and consolidate the republic, it follows that the first rule of our political conduct should be to relate all our activities to the maintenance of equality and the development of virtue.'[23]

In these remarks, Robespierre was not advocating economic equality. Despite a clear sympathy for the popular masses and at least some of their demands, there is no coherent social progamme attributable to Robespierre and his fellow Jacobins; certainly not an egalitarian one.[24] The equality Robespierre advocated was equality of citizenship, equality before the law, equality as a constituent part of the sovereign. According to *The Social Contract*, all citizens are to count equally as voters and the laws they enact are to be unbiased (with respect to individuals) in what they proscribe or enjoin.[25] If, in the force of circumstances, Robespierre violated the first of these formulae, allowing assemblies of delegates to replace the assembled people, he was faithful to the intentions of both. In the Republic of Virtue, everyone *qua* citizen is equal no matter what 'merely' private differences, including differences of wealth and class, remain.

In the end, it is equality of moral personality that Robespierre, following Rousseau, declared the meaning (*sens*) of the Republic. Like Rousseau's, his republicanism assumed a proto-Kantian dimension, according human beings dignity (*Würde*) and therefore unconditional respect. Then virtue is the condition for preserving parties to the social contract 'in the spirit of their institutions' (Rousseau) or, what comes to the same thing, the 'principle' of popular government (Robespierre).[26] Where virtue reigns, private interest is overcome. Virtue is the general will become flesh. It is the realization in human beings of liberty and equality.

If Rousseauean political philosophy is indeed incapable of comprehending revolutionary processes and revolutionary governments, we should expect this incapacity to become evident around the notion of virtue. For virtue is the practical expression, the embodiment in persons, of the philosophical apparatus Rousseau brings to bear for theorizing the state. It is not surprising, then, that with regard to virtue, Robespierre and his comrades found themselves obliged to deny in practice, what, as declared followers of Rousseau, they fervently advocated in theory.

Terror

We have seen how Robespierre cannot have had a Rousseauean 'dictatorship' in mind when he insisted that 'the mainspring of popular government in time of revolution is virtue and terror combined'. It should now be evident that a politics that would combine terror with virtue cannot be accommodated at all within Rousseau's conceptual framework. There would be moral peril, but no conceptual difficulty, if terror were advocated for use against persons outside the state and opposed to it. But Robespierre plainly intended otherwise. Terror, Robespierre insisted, is a principle of revolutionary government itself. Revolutionary governments govern through terror.

Robespierre's conjuction of virtue and terror is paradoxical because a reign of terror, directed internally, betokens an absence of virtue. Where terror is necessary, private wills still hold sway. But the virtuous are virtuous precisely for having subordinated their private wills to the general will. Thus Robespierre's formula restates the paradox of sovereignty, according to which the condition for the possibility of the *de jure* state is the termination of its reason for being as a state. In *The Social Contract*, the paradox passes notice in consequence of an equivocation: states grounded in force and states that only use force strategically — to overcome their collective weaknesses of will — are systematically confounded. In effect, Robespierre exposed this equivocation and the apparent consistency it allows, insisting that, at least for revolutionary governments, states can only be grounded in force. Terror, after all, is just the force of the state writ large. In declaring terror a principle of revolutionary government, Robespierre declared virtue and therefore sovereignty itself grounded in force.

But Robespierre's formula is important for more than just what it suggests about Rousseau's political philosophy. Robespierre was a political actor, not a political philosopher, and if he contrived paradoxes in a Rousseauean idiom, it was not so much to elaborate a theoretical position as to articulate a sense of the politics in which he and his fellow Jacobins were engaged. Implicitly, Robespierre did discover the paradox of Rousseauean sovereignty and the equivocation on which Rousseau's 'resolution' depends. But what matters even more is his use of this paradox, no doubt unwittingly, to introduce a new and momentuous category into political philosophy: the idea of a revolutionary state — a state that, through its proper form of government, directs a transition from one social order to another.

Robespierre does seem to have conceived revolutionary government expressly as a mere transitional form. The conjuction of virtue and terror was to be a stage on the road to a reign of virtue unblemished by terror. However Robespierre recognized that revolutionary government, though transitional, is not, like a Rousseauean dictatorship, a temporary suspension of sovereignty. Rather, it is a governmental form in its own right, signalling the existence of a yet unrecognized type of state. The difference is not just a theoretical nicety. It is a call for a reorientation of Rousseauean thought. Rousseau's political philosophy explores eternal forms. The state described in *The Social Contract* is real whether or not it has ever been realized on earth or ever will be. Robespierre, in reflecting on and intervening in revolutionary events in process effectively historicized Rousseau's vision, turning Rousseauean political philosophy away from the world of Platonic ideas towards the real world of politics in a revolutionary age.

We should not be surprised that Robespierre offered no Rousseauean justification for terror. There is none to be offered. Instead, in Rousseauean fashion, he could only assert a paradox, drawn with particular acuity for rhetorical and heuristic effect. In the past, terror had been used, systematically or capriciously, to maintain private interests ('the laws of tyrants'). However for the revolutionary government Robespierre led, it is intended as an instrument for wiping out private interests, for creating citizens. Terror, Robespierre maintained, 'is not so much a principle in itself as a consequence of the general principle of democracy, applied to the most urgent needs of the nation'. But the 'general principle of democracy' is the exercise of the general will made flesh in the virtue of its citizens. Then terror cannot be a consequence of virtue, no matter what the needs of the nation. For where the nation — 'the moral and collective body' of (virtuous) citizens — exists, private interest does not; and terror lacks a sufficient reason. In short, Robespierre's version of Rousseau's paradox is without even apparent resolution. Virtue and terror cannot be joined in the same conceptual space.

To comprehend their own practice theoretically, the Jacobins evidently needed to effect a further revolution: a revolution in political theory. They were not, however, disposed or able to execute this conceptual revolution. The most they could do was reveal the need for it and — in paradoxical declarations — venture a few halting steps towards its emergence.

What the Jacobins Discovered

Virtue and terror cannot be joined in Rousseauean theory, though they can — and sometimes must — be joined in a revolutionary practice that is properly Rousseauean in its inspiration and objectives. In drawing this conclusion implicitly, Robespierre and his fellow Jacobins effectively identified a flaw in Rousseau's political philosophy. What they discovered, in short, is that Rousseau had misconstrued the fundamental constituents of political life; that his 'ontology' was wrong.

For Rousseau, there exist only two kinds of interest, private and general, and corresponding to these interests, two kinds of will: the private will (which aims at a private interest) and the general will (which aims at the general interest). Politics is a struggle between these wills. As a first approximation, the struggle is over institutions and their tendencies — for the conquest of 'opinion'. Ultimately, however, the site of struggle is internal to each individual — between that which is rational (and aims at the general interest) and that which is not. Private interest is the interest of individuals in a state of nature. It is the will of the individual as a non- or (to keep Rousseau's quasi-historical metaphor) pre-citizen. On the other hand, the general will is the will of the individual as a citizen, as an equal and indivisible member of the sovereign. There are, then, only individuals in Rousseau's political ontology, considered under two aspects of 'forms of association': as independent 'atoms' in a state of nature or as indivisible constituents of the *de jure* state. There is nothing else.

What, then, of voluntary associations not founded on a contract of total alienation: guilds, trade associations, unions, political parties? And what of more or less involuntary associations — social classes, religious sects, racial and ethnic groupings — that also generate interests affecting individuals' will? Rousseau's theory of sovereignty countenances neither sort of group. All 'forms of association' less than the state itself are assimilated into the ontological category of individuals in the state of nature — with merely private interests. In putting an end to the state of nature, the social contract ends any and all associations that fall short of the state itself.[27] And what is denied in theory is then suppressed in practice. Any properly Rousseauan politics, whether concocted for the ideal state of *The Social Contract* or for the imperilled state of the French republic, is motivated by this exigency.

Of course, the sorts of interests Rousseau denied in theory and proscribed in practice do exist — stubbornly and, for all appearances, inexorably. It is indeed the existence of these interests — and the social groupings that generate them — that makes revolutionary transformations possible. To make their theory accord with the reality they faced, the French revolutionaries had either to change their theory or to change their world. Rousseau, we have seen, attempted the latter course, at least in theory: to establish sovereignty, he imagined a transformed social reality. Hence the operations he proposed for implementing solidarity and equality or, in a word, for instilling virtue. Hence too his economic proposals for a classless and prosperous society. In spirit if not always to the letter, allowing for differences in time and place and for the urgency of their situation, the radical Jacobins followed Rousseau. Thus they moved to suppress partial associations: the Le Chapelier law of 14 June 1791 banned workers' organizations; feudal privileges were frequently the subject of prohibitive legislation and in July of 1793 were summarily proscribed; and the establishment of the Cult of the Supreme Being, in the penultimate month of the revolutionary government (June 1794), with Robespierre as its Head and Rousseau's civil religion its inspiration, attempted to deliver the *coup de grâce* to the Roman Catholic Church in France. None of these measures were entirely successful and some were plain failures. All, however, were moves in the direction of implementing Rousseau's ontology. They were misguided perhaps and even futile, but still appropriate in principle for the theory Rousseau proposed and the politics it suggested.

However, it became readily apparent that offending social groups — particularly those that are not voluntary associations — are not susceptible to reforms of this sort. They cannot be conjured away juridically or abolished by legislative fiat. Jacobin practice ultimately foundered on this stubborn fact and a nearly total theoretical incapacity for addressing it. Marx would, of course, privilege class divisions in accounting for historical change and also for theorizing political forms and their futures. In Part 2, this theoretical orientation will be defended. Rousseau's Jacobin critics hardly anticipated historical materialism and, like Rousseau, lacked a clear conception of class. But they did, implicitly, acknowledge a decisive role for social classes and their struggles in social revolutions.

We have seen how Rousseau too was sensitive, implicitly, to the danger class divisions pose for the *de jure* state. But we know that his plans for addressing this danger were hopelessly utopian. In the midst of the dissolution of European feudalism, a simple yeoman society structured by republican institutions was not an historical possibility. Revolutionary France was a society riven by internal divisions. In anticipation of Marxian claims and on the basis of generations of corroborating historical research, I submit that what were decisive in revolutionary France were class divisions, and that class struggles shaped the dynamic of the revolutionary process the Jacobins attempted to direct. In the face of this *historical* reality, philosophical denial and utopian reform, the twin contributions of Rousseauean philosophy, were plainly impotent.

Although Robespierre and his comrades *thought* as Rousseaueans and therefore *spoke* in the name of humanity in general, the revolutionary government they led — and, above all, the brutal Terror they conducted — marked an implicit recognition of the intractable reality of class struggle and an attempt, no doubt excessive and misdirected, to develop a politics appropriate to the reality they faced. With the revolutionary government, the Jacobins sought to take charge of a complex and protracted class struggle in process. They became the party not of some putative general will, but for a constellation of popular anti-feudal, anti-aristocratic, and sometimes even anti-bourgeois 'private wills' — wills deemed irrational and pre-political by Rousseau's political philosophy, but efficacious and inexorable nevertheless.

In representing these interests, intentionally or despite themselves, the Jacobins effectively denied Rousseau's political ontology. What the French revolutionaries recognized, without quite realizing they had, is that the assimilation of interests that are not general to private interests in untenable; and nowhere more so than in situations like their own — in revolutions in progress. They discovered that revolutionary politics is not a contest for supremacy between eternally opposed private and general wills, but an historical struggle where classes contend in and over the state. In short, they discovered, again without realizing they had, that an adequate theory of the state and revolution must take classes, not individuals in atomized social relations, as its fundamental constituent.

Rousseau's theory of sovereignty can be adapted only so far for grasping the reality of class struggle. That limit is suggested, effectively, by Robespierre's paradoxical assertion that virtue and terror combined is the principle or 'mainspring' of popular government in time of revolution. Virtue: supposing the generality of the will; that is, the reality of equality and the overcoming of all that divides society. Terror: supposing the persistence of particularity, of wills, representing fundamental social divisions. It will become clear in later chapters why classes are decisive in this historical drama; and why their interests are anything but pre- or non-political. The French Revolution made their reality difficult even for the most dedicated Rousseaueans, to ignore. Robespierre, the revolutionary leader, the great tactician, confronted the reality of class struggle directly. But so far as he remained caught in the web of Rousseauean concepts, he could not conceive the situation clearly and unambiguously. He could only indicate it through an irreducibly paradoxical declaration.

Rousseau's political ontology entails a radical underestimation of the difficulty of overcoming social divisions inimical to the supremacy of the general will; and a corresponding inability to conceive a non-utopian political strategy for eliminating these embarrassments to the theory. However, the politics Rousseau's Jacobin followers practised belies Rousseau's idea of a politics motivated by a general interest, expressing a general will. Explicit declarations to the contrary, the general will played no role in Jacobin politics, except perhaps to indicate — inadequately, but evocatively, and in a congenial, Rousseauean idiom — an ideal to guide a long and arduous process of revolutionary construction.

Jacobin practice, however, raises a host of problems in its own right. The Jacobins were among the first to seek to remake the world on new foundations; and to employ whatever means seemed necessary to achieve the moral regeneration, the virtue, they sought to realize. To many of their contemporaries and to many still today, their work appears well-intentioned, but devastating in its results. Jacobinism, as a paradigm of revolutionary politics, raises to the fore the question of doing ill by seeking to do good. It will be instructive to reflect on these issues before turning to expressly Marxian themes.

4
Revolution and Utopia

In the late twentieth century, in a world transformed in the aftermath of the French Revolution, hardly anyone regards this event as an unqualified disaster or even, on balance, as an unfortunate occurrence. Historical judgement has not been so kind, however, to the revolutionary government Robespierre led. Few today would deny the need for extraordinary measures in defence of the Revolution in the years 1793-4, and few would deny the good intentions that moved Robespierre and his fellow Jacobins. Yet the consequence of these well-intentioned, extraordinary measures was the Terror — what popular and also philosophical imagination has come to regard with horror. The Terror was, by nearly all accounts, an evil. But was it a necessary evil and, if so, what are we then to make of the Revolution itself?

I will not be concerned at all with differing judgements about the Terror's severity nor with other assessments of the revolutionary government's programs. It seems clear from an abundance of evidence provided by later revolutionary ventures that excess is a temptation to which revolutionary governments, like human beings generally, all too readily succumb. It is therefore a question of some moment — for revolutionaries as well as for those who would learn from them or assess them — to determine what, in particular circumstances, is excessive. This issue cannot fail to arise even in strictly philosophical discussions. However, it cannot be settled by fiat. Since charges of revolutionary excess are always directed against particular measures, they raise questions for which only concrete, historical evidence can be decisive. Thus no prospective position on the Terror, nor on measures undertaken elsewhere by other revolutionary regimes, can be teased out of Rousseau's political writings. This is not simply because these developments were unforeseen by Rousseau but because there is little helpful to say at the level of abstraction at which Rousseau thought about politics philosophically. What can be extracted from Rousseau are views that bear on revolutionary politics in general. In this sense, Rousseau did address, though indirectly, the question of the justifiability of the evils revolutionary governments necessarily promote, as opposed to the arguably avoidable evils actual revolutionary regimes have in fact promoted.

Rousseau's view of social revolution was characteristically ambivalent. On the one hand, by stressing the importance of circumstance and tradition, Rousseau anticipated a strain of conservative theorizing developed by Tocqueville and, before him, by Burke, directed expressly against the likes of Robespierre, according to which it is held that great and unnecessary evils are sure to result whenever radical breaks with received institutional arrangements, practices and customs are attempted. On the other hand, Rousseau advanced a way of thinking about politics that is nothing if not radical, that implicitly supports revolutionary breaks with old regimes, and that accords well with the hope all revolutionaries cherish — to build a new world on the ashes of the old. As already remarked, Rousseau exhibits both what Pascal called *l'esprit de finesse* and also *l'esprit de géométrie*: a sense of politics as an art, developed over time, not according to universally applicable rules but in response to particular problems in particular circumstances; and, at the same time, the conviction that politics, like geometry, is grounded on timeless first principles. In political matters, *l'esprit de finesse* seems tendentiously conservative and anti-revolutionary, supposing the existing order to embody a certain wisdom that only the foolish would jeopardize. *L'esprit de geometrie* in politics is, in contrast, the spirit of revolution itself. Whoever would ground politics on first principles must be prepared to replace the actual with the ideal by overthrowing whatever does not accord with the principles prescribed.

It might seem that this ambivalence is a consequence of the fruitful but ultimately inconsistent juxtaposition of conceptual frameworks distinguished in chapter 1: that it is as a Kantian that Rousseau promoted *l'esprit de géométrie* in politics (human autonomy serving as the ultimate ground for the *de jure* state), and as a non-Kantian that he valued tradition and continuity and anticipated conservative and even anti-revolutionary positions on revolutionary politics. This impression has merit, but it is partial and misleading. Despite what may at first appear, a sensitivity to the place of *l'esprit de finesse* in politics need not support opposition to political and social revolution.

I will argue, in fact, that *l'esprit de finesse* is indispensable for any revolutionary politics that expects plausibly to produce outcomes consonant with the intentions that motivate it. Revolutionaries should therefore be conservatives too, the better to make revolutions. But not conservatives like those who populate the contemporary political landscape. The conservatism I have in mind instead, the conservatism of Tocqueville and Burke and of Rousseau, shorn of its partisanship for the status quo, contains a 'rational kernel' revolutionaries would do well to heed.

To gain a purchase on the lesson conservatism offers revolutionaries, it will be useful to reflect on conservatism generally, and briefly too on Tocqueville's and Burke's assessments of the revolution in France. The understanding of politics that will emerge develops an aspect of Rousseauean political theory that supplements the general bearings historical materialism provides; and that, joined with these and other Marxian claims, helps support the possibility of realizing a republic of ends on earth.

Conservatism

In political discourse in the United States and with important local variations in other advanced capitalist countries, 'conservatism' has come to stand for a variety of positions and attitudes only distantly related to the conservatism implicit in Rousseauean thought and in the writings of Tocqueville and Burke. It is tempting to designate Tocqueville's and Burke's conservatism the true variety and to impugn what the term has come to stand for nowadays as a corruption of the genuine article. Were philosophical interest the sole criterion, it would be justified to succumb to the temptation. However, in applying political designations, usage must count for something. If only to dispel potential misunderstandings then, some attention must be paid to conservatism in its current uses. This burden is discharged, briefly, in Appendix 1.

The conservatism of Tocqueville and Burke rests, very generally, on two claims: having to do with the nature of politics as an activity, and with the risks of innovation in political affairs. Proponents of the one view typically hold the other too; and the first view can be adduced in (partial) support of the second.

Conservatives follow Rousseau in emphasizing the role of *l'esprit de finesse* in politics. In the conservative view, politics is an art, not susceptible to rational reconstruction or mechanical description. The investigation of 'foundations' in political theory is therefore suspect from the start, as are views of politics grounded in 'first principles'. An epistemological analogue of everything political conservatism abhors is Descartes' investigation in the *Meditations on First Philosophy* of all received judgements – with a view to discovering certainties upon which scientific knowledge and religious belief might be reconstructed. Cartesian doubt epitomizes the rationalist's audacity and faith in Reason's capacity to find conceptual bearings and guide practice. Unfettered Reason takes precedence even over the accumulated wisdom of common sense and received beliefs. For the conservative, Rationalism, whatever its merits in certain domains – in the sciences, for instance, or in geometry and 'first philosophy' – is radically inappropriate for politics. Instead, caution is advised and accumulated wisdom is considered the only trustworthy guide.

Politics, conservatives hold, is like cooking or carpentry or architecture. There is no generally correct way to cook or to build a cabinet or a house. Practices develop over time and are peculiar to times, places and circumstances. Some practices, of course, are better than others. And within particular traditions and styles, there are not only better and worse but also right and wrong ways to perform particular tasks. However right and wrong in these contexts is not a matter of deduction from first principles, but of respect for established practices. There is no right and wrong apart from particularities of context and circumstance and, in general, no place for *l'esprit de géométrie*.[1]

Conservatives also claim that changes, particularly radical changes, are inordinately risky and ought therefore to be undertaken with the utmost caution, if at all. In Appendix 2, I will sketch a characteristic defence of conservative caution, appealing to the view of human nature attributed, in Chapter 1, to St Augustine and Hobbes. But caution can be defended regardless of views about human beings' capacities for good or ill. Insofar as the tasks at hand remain roughly as they have been, received ways of setting about these tasks will be at least adequate. By continuing the status quo or changing only slightly, we are unlikely to do much worse than we have already done. The way things have been done is almost certainly not the best way conceivable. But the fear of doing worse overrides expectations of fundamental improvements.

A high degree of aversion to risk is not just an accident of temperament but a reasonable posture in domains, like affairs of state, where mistakes can be devastatingly costly. Even so, conservative caution can be overridden. Sometimes the old ways don't work even tolerably well. Then conservatism will have diminished appeal and caution will compete with a desire for change. If conditions are right, caution will lose in the competition. In principle, therefore, even dedicated conservatives can become revolutionaries. But the tendency of conservatism is against any fundamental assault on the status quo. Received practices and institutions are the conservative's ballast against going drastically wrong.

The tendency of Rationalism is diametrically opposed. Rationalism suggests a politics of overthrow and reconstruction – a determination to grasp politics by the root. There are many more Rationalists among political theorists than conservatives. Still, as noted, a conservative attitude predominates in political life. In short, the ambivalence Rousseau's political thinking exhibits is reproduced and generalized throughout existing political communities. The predominance of conservative attitudes in actual politics and in the attitudes and practices even of individuals who are not philosophically conservative attests to a core insight in the conservative vision.

The point, again, is not that change is unwise. Nor is it that radical change can never be beneficial. Typically, conservatives believe that radical changes will issue in grave misfortunes and produce few tangible benefits. But all conservatives need hold is that far-reaching changes are likely to generate fewer benefits than costs. This sense of the matter follows, in part, from the conviction that politics is not amenable to rationalist strictures but, like cooking, carpentry or architecture, to development grounded in tradition. However, this is not the place to pursue the various and subtle rationales conservative political philosophers have adduced for caution. What is pertinent here is not conservative political philosophy, but the sense of politics conservatism conveys. The idea that politics is an art in which slow, plodding wisdom takes precedence over rationalist audacity — and in which caution and continuity are preeminent values — has important consequences for philosophical treatments of the state and revolution and, ironically, even for defending the possibility of statelessness under communism. But we should take care in specifying what these consequences are and avoid exaggerating their implications.

Revolution in France: Tocqueville, Burke, Rousseau

That the French Revolution, in its positive aspects, only continued transformations well under way in pre-Revolutionary France is the central thesis of Alexis de Tocqueville's study of pre-Revolutionary France, *The Old Regime and the French Revolution.*[2] Feudal society, in Tocqueville's view, was in the process of dissolution and a centralized, rationally administered nation state was already emerging. The definitive triumph of bourgeois society was largely accomplished before the Revolution.

Tocqueville therefore concluded that the French Revolution resulted in far less of a break from the *ancien régime* than is commonly supposed. To be sure, the express intent of many of the more radical revolutionaries was, in Cartesian fashion, to build a new world on new foundations. However, Tocqueville notes:

> 'I have always felt that they were far less successful in this curious attempt than is generally supposed in other countries and that they themselves at first believed. For I am convinced that though they had no inkling of this, they took over from the old regime not only most of its customs, conventions, and modes of thought, but even those very ideas which prompted our revolutionaries to destroy it; that, in fact, though nothing was further from their intentions, they used the debris of the old order for building up the new.'[3]

Tocqueville would concede that the Revolution hastened changes already underway and that many of these changes were historically progressive. It was hardly a reactionary nostalgia for feudalism that prompted Tocqueville's hesitations. Rather Tocqueville faulted the revolutionaries for their radicalism, contending that the Revolution's achievements were accomplished at an enormous and unnecessary cost. What the French lost, far more than need be, was liberty of the kind Tocqueville saw flourishing in America and even in England, the spirit of independence in the face of custom and authority.[4] Liberty in this sense was, in Tocqueville's view, a value in its own right. It is also, Tocqueville argued, a necessary condition for democracy. In its absence, democratic forms become disguises for despotism and individuals degenerate into subservient and dominated beings. The French revolutionaries were therefore right to struggle for liberty. Nevertheless the Revolution they waged had, in large measure, turned into its opposite.

Tocqueville's explanation for this unfortunate reversal is complex and subtle. The assault on traditional practices abruptly shattered the social bonds and solidarities that constituted French society.[5] In consequence, the social and political institutions the revolutionaries built to take the place of those they had overthrown were ripe for despotic usurpation. Liberty, in Tocqueville's view, requires a settled social context for sustenance and growth. It requires a sense of place and, therefore, a character type not easily cultivated in a fragmented, mass society. Thus despite what Tocqueville would readily concede – that the old order was still substantially rife with obstacles to freedom – the atomization of the social order of the *ancien régime*, the inevitable consequence of revolution in France, was inimical to one of the principal ideals for which the *ancien régime* was revolutionized.

Liberty was for Tocqueville what civil order was for Augustine and Hobbes: the supreme achievement of human association – continually in peril and always to be defended. Thus wisdom requires caution in approaching whatever might jeopardize this value. Attacks on established patterns of social cohesion are therefore particularly suspect. Radicalism is unwise, moreover, when as Tocqueville thought of the *ancien régime*, established practices were already evolving in a way that revolution might, at best, only accelerate. In short, the French revolutionaries were at fault for their imprudent and even dangerous impatience with the pace of change; not, in the main, for the kinds of changes they sought to promote.

This criticism is formal in the sense that it does not directly address the content of the measures the French revolutionaries proposed. It might be applied to any politics aiming at the radical transformation of institutions moving, albeit slowly, in the right direction. The general idea is that the social conditions required for liberty to flourish — community and a concommitant sense of place — are needlessly jeopardized by radicalism, and that, despite all good intentions, revolutionary ventures, except perhaps in the direst of circumstances, are inimical to what revolutions are made for.

In addition, Tocqueville did question the tendency of French revolutionary politics, particularly in its more radical, egalitarian phases. He was less sanguine even than Robespierre about the merits of promoting equality. But Tocqueville's attitude towards egalitarianism is not the issue here.[6] It will suffice to acknowledge what readers of *The Old Regime and the French Revolution* cannot mistake: a plain reluctance on Tocqueville's part to applaud uncritically many of the measures the revolutionaries took on behalf of equality. In calling attention to putative conflicts between liberty and equality and examining some of its consequences, Tocqueville anticipated an attitude implicit in much subsequent political philosophy, conservative and otherwise. There is nothing conservative, however, in favouring liberty over other values with which it might conflict. Quite the contrary, as Augustine's and Hobbes's evident preference for order over other values, including freedom, illustrates. The distinctively conservative aspect of Tocqueville's assessment of the French Revolution is, again, the formal judgement — the claim that the revolutionaries set about their tasks with unwarranted impatience and with an inappropriate enthusiasm for 'going to the root'. Tocqueville's more substantive judgements about particular programmes revolutionaries pursued raise questions of another sort.[7]

The formal, conservative judgement is pressed with particular force and perspicuity in Edmund Burke's contemporary *Reflections on the Revolution in France.*[8] Burke exceeded Tocqueville in questioning egalitarian values, though his strictures against this revolutionary ideal characteristically lacked the subtlety of Tocqueville's. And he joined Tocqueville in an appreciation of the spirit of liberty that encouraged the American Revolution and was fostered by its success. Still, in Burke's writings, the emphasis is straightforwardly on the perils of breaking abruptly with established practices and arrangements. The argument is by now familiar. Burke bears special mention not just because of his celebrity as a critic of the French Revolution, but for the bold generality with which he asserted the conservative case. Tocqueville questioned the wisdom of revolutionary ruptures in consequence of the dangers revolutions pose for liberty. Burke, however, faulted revolutionary practice and advocated conservatism not just for liberty's sake, but on more general grounds.

His rationale is nowhere explicitly asserted, but is implied by nearly everything he wrote in the *Reflections*. Thus he argued that by breaking radically with received traditions and practices, whether or not the old ways were defective and in need of reform, the French revolutionaries incurred inordinately grave risks. To restate the point anachronistically: the expected utility of the benefits of revolutionary change fell far short of the expected disutility of the costs. It is instructive to note that Burke's reasons for believing in the wisdom of risk aversity in political affairs do not stem from any dark view of human nature and the human condition. In fact, Burke was Whiggishly optimistic in his reflections on human potentialities.[9] His advocacy of caution and his distaste for radicalism stem, instead, from his conception of the nature of politics. Thus Burke, like Tocqueville, effectively joined that side of Rousseau's thought that insists upon the fundamentally conjunctural character, the essential historicity, of politics.

What Tocqueville and Burke opposed, above all, is *l'esprit de géométrie* in politics, the tendency to concoct political and social arrangements by appeal to Reason, without proper regard for circumstance and history. Burke stated this opposition directly, in terms no less emphatic than Rousseau's.

> 'Circumstances (which with some gentlemen pass for nothing) give in reality to every political principle its distinguishing colour, and discriminating effect. The circumstances are what render every civil and political scheme beneficial or noxious to mankind.'[10]

And he went on, throughout the *Reflections*, to fault the French revolutionaries precisely for approaching political matters as geometricians, even to the point of using mathematical techniques to address political problems.[11] The revolutionaries, Burke contended, were clever when they ought to have been wise.

Tocqueville, writing with the advantage of fifty years of distance from which to view the Revolution and also eighteenth-century France, was no less critical of the tendency of the French revolutionaries to approach political questions in the manner of eighteenth-century philosophers concerned with abstract speculation and first principles:

> 'When we closely study the French Revolution we find that it was conducted in precisely the same spirit as that which gave rise to so many books expounding theories of government in the abstract. Our revolutionaries had the same fondness for broad generalizations, cut-and-dried legislative systems, and a pedantic symmetry; the same contempt for hard facts; the same taste for reshaping institutions on novel, ingenious, original lines; the same desire to reconstruct the entire constitution according to the rules of logic and a preconceived system instead of trying to rectify its faulty parts.'[12]

And Tocqueville was clear in his assessment of the consequences: 'The result was nothing short of disastrous; for what is a merit in the writer may well be a vice in the statesman and the very qualities which go to make great literature can lead to catastrophic revolutions.'[13]

Here, in short, is the Rousseauean view of politics or, more precisely, the view of its non-Kantian component, invoked in opposition to a revolution made, in part, to realize a vision inspired by Rousseau's work; a revolution that sought, so far as possible, to create political forms approximating the institutions proposed in *The Social Contract.* It is as though one strain of Rousseau's thought has been turned against the other. However this impression is misleading. Rousseau, like Tocqueville and Burke, was emphatically in opposition to abstraction and, more generally, to Cartesianism in politics. And as Tocqueville's and Burke's examples illustrate, anti-Cartesianism can have conservative and even anti-revolutionary implications. But it need not. Ironically, these anti-revolutionary implications can be rebutted, in part, by appeal to the very insights Tocqueville and Burke adapted to conservative and anti-revolutionary ends.

A sense of the historicity of politics and of the overwhelming importance of local traditions and customs suggests, but does not entail, conservatism and opposition to revolutionary change. The suggestion depends, however, on an unstated assumption, deeply entrenched in the thought of Tocqueville and Burke, implicit also in Rousseau's political theory and throughout mainstream political philosophy. What is assumed is that political systems are in principle immune from systemic factors that elicit radical discontinuities in political institutions. Discontinuities are possible, of course, but they are always deviant or, in the literal sense, extraordinary.[14] Radical breaks may result from the machinations of misguided politicians, as Tocqueville and Burke maintained for revolutionary France. Or they may be responses, misguided or not, to extra-systemic factors like natural calamities or external invasions. In principle, though, gradual and continuous change is the norm. Political institutions evolve unless, contrary to their nature, they are revolutionized.

Neither Tocqueville nor Burke advanced claims about the dynamics of political change. Rousseau's position is somewhat more developed. In his view, political systems, like organisms, proceed, at their own pace, through a sequence of birth, development, decay and dissolution.[15] Rousseau does not proffer developed explanations for these changes, but it can be inferred from what he does say that, in his view, the causes of change in political systems are generally internal to political systems themselves. Since neither Tocqueville nor Burke have any notion of the interconnection of politics with other social or economic arrangements, they too, if only by default, construe political change as an internal, evolutionary affair. It is reasonable to speculate, then, even in the absence of texts that bear directly on the issue, that for all three writers, normal political change is endogenous.

In the chapters that follow, I will show how Marx advanced a quite different view, according to which change is not continuous and gradual 'other things being equal', but discontinuous and, at critical moments in the historical trajectory, abrupt. The dispute is not easily resolved by appealing to historical evidence. Insofar as the motivations of political actors, international rivalries and the vagaries of nature are counted as circumstances that can upset what it is for other things to be equal, the difference between continuity and discontinuity is generally blurred. But there is a difference nevertheless; and its implications are important.

Inasmuch as Rousseau is in accord with Tocqueville and Burke, his view of politics, like theirs, is tendentially conservative and anti-revolutionary. For Tocqueville and Burke, however, a principled opposition to revolutionary politics is the point of their reflections on the French Revolution. Rousseau had no comparable intent. There is indeed another side of Rousseau's thought which suggests a very different attitude, as Robespierre's example attests. Rousseau is a proponent of moral self-realization through politics. It is not so great a step beyond the spirit, if not the letter, of Rousseau's express declarations to opt, as the radical Jacobins did, for moral rejuvenation through revolution. Rousseau, again, had no notion of social revolution. But there is a side of his thought that is more than congenial to the idea.

In Rousseau's thought, these rival perspectives coexist in an uneasy tension. They are not, however, strictly inconsistent. It is possible, as Rousseau's own case attests, to detach conservatism and opposition to revolution from a clear recognition of the historicity of politics, even if it is natural for the latter view to suggest the former in the absence of a theory that makes revolutionary change normal and gradual evolution deviant. The impetus for reversing the thrust of Tocquevillean and Burkean conservatism, for 'standing it on its feet', depends, in short, on extra-Rousseauean theoretical resources; specifically, on a theory of history that confers a dependent theoretical status to political systems and their trajectories.

The Rational Kernel

Conservatism's rational kernel is its insistence on the importance of circumstances and traditions in shaping political practices. Shorn of its characteristic but unnecessary, anti-revolutionary implications, conservatism warns that it is only with an eye to the past — as it shapes and conditions the present — that desired futures, if possible at all, have any hope of realization. Actions, especially political actions, will always have unintended consequences. But if outcomes are to accord at all with intentions, political actors must acknowledge the constraints conservatives stress. Whatever falls outside the bounds of these constraints is utopian.

To combat utopianism, the most urgent need is to account, so far as possible, for what is and is not on the historical agenda; an issue on which conservatism sheds virtually no light. Conservatism calls attention only to means. But in doing so, conservative critics of the French Revolution effectively provided the first significant contribution to a political theory of social revolution before Marx. They identified genres of political practice for which the charge of utopianism is appropriate. They showed too why utopianism is a charge of considerable moment. Conservatives are right to emphasize that politics is a serious business and that wrong moves can have disastrous consequences. And whatever they may themselves have concluded, they demonstrated that utopian styles in politics are destined to result in unhappy outcomes; the outcomes conservatives ascribe to revolutionary pursuits generally. Tocqueville and Burke and sometimes Rousseau stood against ambitious intentions and radical changes. In the chapters that follow, reasons will be marshalled against drawing anti-revolutionary conclusions. But what can be learned from these conservative critics, even so, is the urgency of opposing adventures waged in disregard of the heavy constraints of the past, and the dangers inherent in unrealistically ambitious intentions and revolutionary styles insensitive to received practices and traditions. The conservative insistence that caution is always advised is their enduring legacy, along with their sensitivity to the actual texture of political life.

Following Tocqueville, Burke and even Rousseau, we can concede that there is reason to be wary of revolutionary politics. And there is certainly merit in the claims of these writers and a host of others who have followed them that there is cause to fault past revolutionary ventures — emphatically including much that has transpired in the course of socialist revolutions. But, after Marx, it will be clear that there is no reason to follow conservatives in concluding against these experiences definitively, and no reason to endorse the conservative view of revolutionary change.

The lesson implicit in conservatism's rational kernel will be resumed in Chapters Seven and Eight. Before its implications for defending the communist and anarchist vision of a cooperative social order can be appreciated, it will be necessary first to confront utopianism directly by reflecting, following Marx, on historical possibility and the role of the state in epochal historical change.

Appendix 1: Contemporary Conservatism

In current political discourse, 'conservative' commonly designates a variety of positions on fiscal and monetary policies and also on social and foreign policy. The characterization provided here aims at a level of generality sufficient for including most of what the term has come to designate in current usage while still capturing what is distinctive about the position. Contemporary conservatism bears only a distant affinity to the conservatism of Tocqueville and Burke. It is also of considerably diminished philosophical interest for reasons that will become evident by reflecting briefly on conservatism, as it has come to be understood, in its social context.

In capitalist societies, what weakens capitalism is normally harmful for nearly everyone, at least in the short-run; including those who dominate the political process. It is not surprising, therefore, that mainstream politics in capitalist countries is overwhelmingly pro-capitalist. Even political parties with working-class constituencies and socialist objectives are compelled, by force of circumstance, to pursue policies that, in varying degrees, advance capitalists' interests. Of course, this constraint on policies permits varying degrees of freedom. Some political actors are more directly pro-business than others in the policies they pursue and in their self-representations. In the United States particularly, but also generally throughout the contemporary scene, conservatives in each of their principal varieties, are at the extreme of the political spectrum in their support for business. But contemporary conservatism is not just commercial boosterism. Conservatives are pro-business, characteristically, in a special way.

Conservatives hold that business interests and therefore, in their view, societal interests are best furthered, if not by strict *laissez-faire*, then by some close approximation, that is, by reversion to the political economic policies of capitalism in its ascendancy. Conservatives, therefore, tend to oppose governmental interference with markets and interventions that redistribute wealth or otherwise weaken the dominance of business interests over society and over the political process.[16] Contemporary conservatives are not quite like nineteenth-century liberals, opposed to all restraints on what individuals can do with what they own. But it is, in large measure, the relatively unconstrained freedom capitalists enjoyed before working-class movements arose as a partial counter-force, that today's conservatives admire and seek to conserve.

This commitment to *laissez-faire* has come to be joined, not always easily, with other positions familiar from more traditional European conservatisms. Thus contemporary conservatives are typically more militarist than most of their countrymen, and more inclined to support the exercise of power abroad. This tendency, however, is a recent phenomenon in the United States. Earlier American conservatives were, if not anti-militarist, at least isolationalist in matters of foreign policy.[17] They tended moreover to see military and business interests as opposed (usually with good reason) and to side with the latter against the former. The circumstances of American capitalism after World War II have, of course, changed radically. There is now a widely perceived harmony, grounded in economic reality, between business and the military. It is not surprising, therefore, that an enthusiasm for the military has come to be part of the constellation of views that comprise contemporary conservative thinking in the United States.

There are other views conservatives hold that have less to do with commercial self-interest and that provide some inkling of the view of politics implicit in Tocqueville's and Burke's criticisms of the French revolutionaries. Contemporary conservatives are generally among those most in support of the family (or, more precisely, of an historically particular and highly idealized conception of the family) and of traditional morality. And more than other mainstream political currents, conservatives rally behind the defence of the inherited social order — including its sexual, racial and class divisions. Conservatives generally support a religious presence in public life and 'patriotism' as an essential component of the civil religion.

It is these latter views, to which conservatives are drawn more by temperament than by interest, that bear the most evident affinity with the conservatism Tocqueville, Burke and Rousseau share. For these views exhibit, despite their historical limitations and peculiarities, a sense of the importance of continuity and tradition. The characteristic pro-business stance of contemporary conservatives has a more tenuous connection with this sensitivity. The promotion of commercial interests is, arguably, a suitable conservative objective, but only in circumstances where society itself has long been deeply commercial.

American society (outside the South) fits this description;

and the extension of its particular concerns to other parts of the world is, no doubt, yet another expression of the cultural imperialism that has come to prevail nearly everywhere. Conservatives tend to be deferential towards authority; and in the contemporary world, as in Hobbes's vision of the political order, might effectively makes right. Still, *laissez-faire* capitalism is bound to matter more to American conservatives than to conservatives in different circumstances and with different traditions. European conservatives have a feudal past and its vestiges to conserve. American conservatives have only homesteads, shops and mills. There is no plausible American conservatism with horizons extending back beyond the preeminence of commercial capitalism and its values.

As in so many other domains, the predominance of American influence, even over local conservatisms, is detrimental to political and social well-being. By valorizing predatory commercial interests — now projected on a worldwide scale — and focusing attention away from the rational insights of earlier conservative thought, contemporary conservatism impedes appreciation of the potential contribution of more thoughtful conservatisms to a genuinely progressive and liberating political theory and practice.

Appendix 2: Conservative Political Philosophy

The rational kernel of Tocqueville's and Burke's conservatism can be defended simply by appealing to the inappropriateness of Cartesian rationalism in politics and the support this claim lends for a high degree of risk aversity. Characteristically, however, conservative political philosophers assert a good deal more including, almost always, a deep pessimism about human potentialities and a corresponding sense of the futility of most human endeavours. Since revolutions are typically collective efforts of historical dimensions, aiming at the radical amelioration of social and political conditions, this theoretically motivated pessimism, if sustainable, would count forcefully against revolutionary undertakings. However, characteristic conservative views of humanity's prospects are detachable from claims for the wisdom of caution in the face of change. It will be useful briefly to articulate the pessimism that underlies so much conservative thought in order to fix on its role in motivating the conservative view of politics, but also to appreciate its conceptual detachability.

Conservative political philosophy is resolutely Christian in the sense indicated in Chapter One. Indeed, a prototypical example of this genre of argument is St Augustine's account of the politics of Fallen Man in *The City of God* and throughout his voluminous political writings.[18] Augustine's is a political philosophy that takes Sin seriously. In consequence of Sin, human beings are radically incapable of doing well for themselves either in what matters most, their personal salvation, or in earthly concerns.[19] Human nature is so fundamentally corrupt, so radically incapable of perfection through human efforts (in the absence of unmerited grace), that a strict adherence to existing order — any order — is necessary to save us from ourselves and from each other. For Augustine, the evil that lurks just beneath the fragile surface of the social order threatens to overwhelm and undo any people who would tamper even slightly with the institutions under which they live. At this bleak limit, opposition to revolution — indeed, to far-reaching change in general — becomes a matter of virtual implication. It is not just that the risk of going wrong swamps the likely benefits of fundamental change, but that change of any significant magnitude is sure to unleash disaster.

Augustine's rationale is theological but the root of his conservatism is a view of human nature and its limitations. Conservative political philosophy can therefore dispense with Augustinian theology without altering its assessment of political endeavours and its dire warnings of the evils of upsetting the existing order. It suffices only to secularize the concept of Sin to retain a sense of the futility of attempts at doing well and of the certainty of disaster should the impossible be attempted. In Augustine's view, we can maintain a semblance of order, the Peace of Babylon, but nothing more. The sole alternative to the Peace of Babylon is the war of all against all.

As already remarked, Hobbesian political philosophy is a secularized Augustinianism; a materialism that avers an essentially Augustinian view of human nature. For Hobbes, as for Augustine, the point of political association is to save us from ourselves and from each other by establishing a coercive apparatus capable of coordinating individuals' activities and mitigating their deleterious effects. If unconstrained, individuals' activities would render everyone an enemy to everyone, with all the attendant consequences for collective and individual well-being and even survival.

The position that Augustine and Hobbes articulate with vehemence and perspicuity and that many other conservatives endorse in a more mitigated fashion does entail conservatism in political affairs. But the converse entailment does not hold. It is possible to be conservatively cautious in politics for just the reason nearly everyone is conservative with respect to cooking, carpentry and house building — because of the nature of the activity. What Augustinianism and its secular variants motivate is a sense of the danger of going astray. But we do not need to imagine the unrestrained eruption of Sin on earth or the war of all against all to sense this danger or to recognize the wisdom of caution. If reflecting on politics as an activity and its attendant risks does not suffice, then, following Tocqueville's and Burke's example, there are numerous instances of revolutionary projects gone wrong to reflect upon and to learn from.

Part 2

Prelude to Part 2

Most of the elements of a political philosophy capable of supporting the idea of the end of the state are now in place. To defend against the charge of utopianism and otherwise develop issues Rousseaueans have only broached, however, an account of the social and economic conditions necessary for a system of politics aiming at establishing a republic of ends is urgently required. To this end, Rousseauean theory provides only intimations. A more apt point of departure is Marx's theory of history. In chapters 5 and 6, I therefore turn from the principal concerns of Part One to some of the intricacies and ramifications of historical materialism. This shift of focus is a necessary theoretical preparation for resuming the main thread of my argument in chapters 7 and 8; and for advancing beyond the horizons of Rousseauean thought.

Intimations of a Theory

In the manner of eighteenth-century contractarian philosophers, Rousseau was only apparently concerned with what actually happened in the past. The story he tells in *The Discourse on the Origin of Inequality Among Men*, the so-called *Second Discourse*, is set in the past, and it is natural to regard it as an exercise in historical speculation, innocently unconstrained by what practising historians would nowadays regard as evidence. However it would be misleading to describe *The Second Discourse* as an historical investigation. Rousseau did not recount or explain historical events. His state of nature was not a pre-political, primordial age, but a rational reconstruction of human life in the absence of specifically political relations. In short, what Rousseau did was concoct a story set in the past — to advance a philosophical position by illustration. Like Plato, he constructed a myth.

This myth anticipates two different views of history: the atheoreticism of mainstream contemporary historiography and the genre of theory of which Marx's is, to date, the only well-elaborated example. In contrast to previous philosophies of history, both mainstream historiography and historical materialism aim to discover pertinent, causal determinations for historical events. They differ, however, over what they regard as explicable. Mainstream historiography aims only to account for particular events; historical materialism considers history itself intelligible.

The idea that history as such is intelligible arose in the context of theological, and later secular, philosophies that purported to interpret the past by revealing its meaning. The meaning of events is, of course, relative to particular perspectives. When the interpretive context varies, meanings change accordingly. A definitive account of the meaning of an event therefore supposes a definitive perspective — a 'final' frame of reference. For this reason, philosophies of history that purport to uncover non-relativistic accounts of the significance of the past are teleological. They conceive an 'end' (*telos*) of history in the light of which whatever is historically significant is retrospectively intelligible. Traditional philosophies of history respect this structure. It is evident in St Augustine's account of Providence directing the course of Roman and then world history towards the Final Judgement, in Spengler's view of historical cycles and eternal recurrence, in Comte's theory of the succession of theological, philosophical and finally scientific stages, and in Kant's notion of the progress of (constitutional) freedom. The immediate ancestor and partial inspiration of Marx's theory of history, Hegel's depiction of the Cunning of Reason culminating in the Idea of Freedom, was the last of these great teleological philosophies.

Teleological explanations of the past would compete with mainstream and Marxian explanations only if what the *telos* philosophers impute is somehow construed as a cause in the sense mainstream and Marxian historians acknowledge. It is not clear whether any of the major, teleological philosophers of history are in fact committed to this view. The end of history, more commonly, is conceived as an (Aristotelian) final cause; not an efficient cause, as in standard causal explanations. Thus Hegel ascribed causal efficacy to individual actors' passions and interests, while attaching explanatory importance not to these particular explanations, but to the end towards which the motley of events converges. Strictly speaking, then, Hegelian explanations are compatible with mainstream or Marxian explanations, though it is hard to see what would warrant ascribing explanatory significance to the end of history, insofar as the means by which the end is produced is understood. This is one reason why mainstream historians and Marxists, like natural scientists since the seventeenth century, have eschewed final causes. In consequence, historical events are nowadays understood to be devoid of meaning, except insofar as historians ascribe them. The past can in principle be explained causally and interpreted relative to particular perspectives. Despite Hegel and his predecessors, however, there are no interpretations to be provided 'under the aspect of eternity'.

We will find that mainstream historiographical and Marxian explanations need not compete either. They each provide strictly causal explanations, but of different sorts. What distinguishes them is, again, their respective views about history itself. Historical materialism retains the view that history has an intelligible structure and direction. It is therefore a general theory of history, though not a teleological theory. By denying that history is amenable to any account of its overall structure and direction, mainstream historiography also avoids teleology. In the mainstream view, particular events are in principle explicable, but there is no explanation for the structure and direction of history itself (excluding, of course, the trivial conjunction of all particular explanations). Rousseau joined each of these non-teleological views in a simple (mythological) story.

Individuals in the early state of nature lived in isolation from one another, satisfying their needs and realizing their wants directly from nature. Population was sparse and nature sufficiently abundant to make competition for resources unnecessary. Therefore no material basis for conflict existed; nor was there need for individuals to cooperate in realizing their objectives. The early state of nature was also in accord with human nature or, more precisely, with human nature as it developed in the self-sufficient and happy isolation Rousseau imputed to the first human beings. Like animals generally, individuals were moved by a concern for their own well-being, a basic self-regard (*amour de soi*); but they were not yet Hobbesian egoists, moved by *amour propre*, seeking to accumulate ceaselessly and to dominate everything. Persons were content with their lot. In short, there were neither 'objective' (material) nor 'subjective' (psychological) pressures destabilizing the social order.

The early state of nature might therefore have continued indefinitely, but for a number of fortuitous, technological innovations — in metallurgy principally — that made settled agricultural production possible. These technological developments are, of course, explicable in principle. In Rousseau's story, they have the status mainstream historiography accords to all events. But they were not in any way necessitated. The social order of the early state of nature bore no endogenous pressures for change. It was hardly immune from destabilization, but it did not contain the seeds of its own undoing.

Technological innovation did not suffice to put an end to the early state of nature. That unhappy event required, in addition, a decisive innovation in social relations. Eventually, according to Rousseau, someone set aside a parcel of land and successfully claimed ownership. In so doing, the common stock of land — the domain where isolated individuals hunted and gathered — was diminished and the productivity of land liberated for agricultural production increased. The diminution of the common stock tended to necessitate imitation at the same time that the bounty produced by settled agriculture tended to encourage it. Hunting and gathering eventually ceased to be a viable way of attending to one's own concerns (*amour de soi*). To survive, it became necessary to own land and farm it.

This social innovation was, again, fortuitous. It could have failed to occur. However, the introduction of private property in land was a necessary condition for exploiting the potentialities of agricultural production. In this instance, what was necessary was also sufficient for inaugurating an historical process with momentous consequences. In Rousseau's view, then, it is private property in land, society's principal productive resource that, once established, provides structure and direction to subsequent changes. With this transformation in social relations, a process was set in motion that made later history amenable to a general theory. From that time on, 'the development of inequality among men' became inevitable.

With greater levels of productivity, the world came to sustain a larger population that made ever-increasing demands on ever-diminishing expanses of land. Altogether the stock of consumables rose, but so too did the population and its needs. Relative abundance therefore gave way to relative scarcity, and to conflict over resources. In this way, conditions that make competition inevitable and cooperation possible were socially produced. And human nature, always plastic and dependent on material conditions, adapted accordingly. Individuals became acquisitive and intent on domination; *amour de soi* gave way to *amour propre*, the psychological basis of the private will. These transformations were mutually reinforcing: objective circumstances encouraged subjective motivations that exacerbated conflict over increasingly scarce resources, in turn augmenting and generalizing *amour propre*. Thus an indefinitely sustainable peace grew into an increasingly unstable 'war of all against all'. It is at this point that the argument of *The Social Contract* begins. The state of nature, having developed into a state of war, 'can no longer subsist, and the human race would perish if it did not alter its mode of existence'. The result, we know, is the social contract and its issue: the *de jure* state.

Thus *The Second Discourse* anticipated mainstream historiography in denying a general theory of historical change: the most momentous change in all of human history before the social contract, the introduction of private property in land, is explained in the manner of mainstream historiography. But it also anticipated historical materialism in explaining subsequent historical developments by reference to endogenous processes, grounded in what Marx was to call 'social relations of production' and propelled by technological development. Where Rousseau strayed, from a Marxian point of view, was in having provided too undifferentiated an account of social relations of production to capture the real epochal divisions. However this may be, Rousseau's speculations are only an anticipation of a theory of history, for it was not actual history he depicted but an imaginary history of his own contrivance, concocted as part of a contractarian programme in political philosophy. What the social contract founds — not in time but in right — is an eternal idea.

5
Historical Materialism

Despite the disarming simplicity of Marx's express declarations on history,[1] and the attention historical materialism has lately attracted,[2] the explanatory objectives of Marx's theory of history remain obscure. It is natural to think of historical materialism as a general theory of history, underlying and motivating particular historical explanations including, of course, those advanced by Marx himself. However this understanding is misleading in ways that obstruct a constructive joining of historical materialism and Rousseauean political philosophy. The connection between a theory of history in Marx's sense and particular historical explanations is more complex than is widely supposed.

Marx probably did consider historical materialism applicable in particular historical explanations. But Marx and most Marxists after him entertained extravagant and implausible ambitions for historical materialism. What will be reconstructed here, in any case, is not Marx's express view. However it is a position that retrieves and develops what is conceptually distinctive in Marx's view. I therefore disavow any claim to have discovered what Marx's theory of history really is. I claim only that the positions developed here derive from the theory Marx advanced and retain its core insights.

To grasp the distinctiveness and also the novelty of historical materialism, it will be instructive to focus on the historicity of the theory, on the sense in which it is an historical theory. Approaching historical materialism from this perspective will help to clarify its role in historical explanations. In doing so, it should also help deflate the controversy over whether Marx was or was not a 'technological determinist', an issue on which recent discussions have tended to founder.[3] It should also help, indirectly, to strengthen the case for the plausibility of Marx's theory or, more precisely, some descendant of it by showing how its core remains robust under a variety of mitigations of its explanatory pretensions. Above all, it will allow us to focus on what (Rousseauean) political philosophy needs in a theory of history in order to conceive the end of the state.

Historical Materialism

The principal objective of historical materialism is to discern the causal determinations that govern the structure and direction of historical change. In explaining by discerning causes, historical materialist explanations are unlike explanations proffered by traditional philosophies of history. However, like its predecessors, historical materialism does claim that the changes it aims to account for are developmental in character and have a determinate directionality. Historical change augments the rate of development of productive forces. Thus historical materialism is an optimizing theory.[4]

Optimizing theories are familiar in well-established scientific research agendas. For instance, the theory of evolution by natural selection refers to the process by which animals and plants best adapted to their environment tend to survive. However the fact that a particular trajectory would optimize the ability to adapt to certain conditions does not cause the system to follow that trajectory. Evolutionary theory, like 'extremal' theories in physics, construes optimization as a consequence of a causal mechanism that also produces the changes in question. That a given change in gene frequencies increases the ability of living things to adapt does not explain why gene frequencies change. Rather, natural selection has two consequences: evolution — a change in gene frequencies — and, in addition, an increase in the quantity optimized. Thus evolutionary theory does not impute 'foresight' to the systems it describes; nor does it maintain that future states of these systems determine present states. In short, it is not a teleological theory in a sense that would compete with standard causal theories.[5] Similarly, the fact that historical materialism depicts societies optimizing the rate of development of productive forces does not render the theory teleological. Historical materialism avoids teleology by deploying a conceptual structure similar, in pertinent respects, to Darwinian evolutionary theory and other well-established optimizing theories.

Historical materialism provides an account of processes that govern the structure and direction of human history. The theory purports to explain the distinguishing features of epochal historical divisions — conceived as discrete economic forms or structures, traditionally designated 'modes of production' — and the conditions for their emergence. Then it is claimed, in addition, that these modes of production explain legal and juridical 'superstructures' and even 'forms of consciousness' (ideologies). Since my concern here is primarily with the dynamic processes the theory postulates, I will focus mainly on the explanations provided for changes in modes of production. The relation of the 'economic base' to superstructural and ideological components of social formations will be a theme of Chapters 7 and 8.

Very generally, Marx held that 'forces of production' tend to develop continuously, bringing about discontinuous transformations of 'social relations of production' where 'forces of production' (or, alternatively, 'productive forces') designate the physical, social and even scientific means at a society's disposal for the appropriation from nature of products of labour; 'social relations of production' (or 'production relations') designate effective, as opposed to strictly juridical, ownership rights over productive resources i.e. forces of production and also persons. Depending on the level of development of the forces of production, a given type of production relation facilitates or impedes ('fetters') the development of productive forces. When production relations fetter development, forces and relations of production are in a structurally unstable configuration. This structural instability is the material condition for epochal change, for the reorganization of social relations of production into new modes of production.

Orthodox historical materialism postulates a unique sequence of discrete economic structures corresponding to different levels of development of productive forces. It then claims that history tends to move through this sequence. Discrete economic structures, different sets of production relations, give rise, moreover, to different forms of class domination. Therefore, what accomplishes the pattern and sequence historical materialism postulates is class struggle — ultimately, in and over social relations of production. In the orthodox view, these struggles are inexorable and their outcomes predictable. The class best suited, at a particular level of development of productive forces, for further developing productive forces will ultimately prevail. Thus there is selection for that set of production relations that is optimal for further developing productive forces.[6] For orthodox historical materialists, then, the possibility of change along the depicted trajectory is, in the long run, sufficient for the indicated change to occur. Where there is a trans-historical human interest in transforming economic structures to unfetter the forces of production, the requisite class capacities develop and social relations of production will be transformed accordingly. At the level of abstraction at which it is pitched — where historical epochs, not particular events, are the proper *explananda* — orthodox historical materialism is therefore a theory of historical inevitability, of an inexorable sequencing of epochal stages.

Historical materialism advances a claim about the lawlike character of change in its proper domain. It claims what *would* happen wherever the conditions under which it has application obtain, and wherever there are no interferences of sufficient force to countervail the effects of historical materialist development. It will be useful, therefore, to distinguish general laws from historical hypotheses that assert the applicability of these laws to the actual world. Insofar as Marx's theory of history purports to provide an account of actual history, historical materialists are committed not only to the general laws historical materialism advances, but also to the claim that these laws do indeed apply in a recognizable way and to a significant extent. But as a general theory, historical materialism can withstand attacks on the historical hypotheses to which its adherents are committed.

Historical materialism's laws provide an account: (a) of necessary material conditions for change according to which, what is possible depends on the level of development of productive forces; (b) of the direction of change (since economic structures change to maximize the rate of development of productive forces and are therefore cumulative and irreversible); (c) of the means through which change is accomplished, i.e.

class struggle; and, finally, (d) of sufficient conditions for change (since what is possible is, in the long run, necessary). Not all of these claims are equally plausible: (d), in particular, is very doubtful, as we shall go on to see. However, the orthodox version of historical materialism, whatever its implausibilities, illustrates clearly the distinctive historicity of historical materialism. It will therefore be convenient, for the present, to ignore non-orthodox variants of the general theory.

Macro/Micro

Evolutionary biologists and practising historians aim at explaining particular events; not major historical trends or epochal transformations. Historical materialism, on the other hand, is a theory of trends and transformations. The explanations evolutionary biologists and practising historians provide are therefore fine-grained. Historical materialist explanations are coarse-grained. Historical materialism is a macro-theory while evolutionary theory and mainstream historiography have little, if any, insight to provide at the macro-level.

The difference can be made clearer by reflecting on the contrast between historical materialism and evolutionary biology. The conceptual apparatus developed in population genetics allows the computation of the evolutionary trajectory of a population (or the probability distribution of possible trajectories) once the values of a specified set of parameters have been determined. Geneticists can then compute the changes in gene frequencies that will occur, given particular evolutionary forces. In this way, changes of gene frequencies within populations, micro-evolutionary changes, are explained. However, population genetics says nothing about large-scale changes in life's diversity. Major changes are understood as cumulative effects of small-scale changes. In principle, anything that can happen in evolution can be represented formally. Evolutionary biologists can therefore describe major transformations. But evolutionary theory provides no special insight into these changes and gives no account of their structure or underlying dynamic.

It is easy to see why evolutionary theory has so little to contribute to the understanding of macro-evolutionary events. If natural selection is indeed the preeminent evolutionary force, change is mainly the result of exogenous, usually environmental, factors. Organisms change to track their environments. Selection will then produce small changes in gene frequencies on a time-scale of relatively few generations. When this process continues throughout the millions of years during which life has and probably will exist on earth, the outcome is largely indeterminate. Inasmuch as environmental change is itself highly variable in space and time, considerable diversity and very little overall pattern will result. Organisms will be assembled fortuitously and the collection of organisms, the totality of life, will be an accidental hodge-podge.

For standard evolutionary theory, then, the major epochs of natural history are 'accidents'. In principle, of course, these changes can be explained, given enough information about gene frequencies and the required parameter values. But evolutionary biologists have no distinct explanation for the trajectory of change itself. Darwinism construes epochs — the Age of Dinosaurs, for example, or the Age of Mammals — in the way non-Marxian historians regard, say, the emergence of capitalism: as the fortuitous result of an accumulation of small-scale changes.

Practising historians share the evolutionary biologist's focus on the particular. They too provide fine-grained explanations, depicting macro-events and trends as accidental consequences of micro-events. But there is a difference. Most historians would deny that any systematic, general theory accounts for particular historical explanations. Historians have no analogue to natural selection. As already noted, mainstream historiography is essentially atheoretical. Every change can be explained causally, at least in principle; but there is no general principle governing historical change and no systematic joining of particular explanations that bears explanatory interest.

'History,' then, can designate anything in the past. There are no constraints on what can count as an historical event except that it has already occurred, and no constraints on the sorts of explanations historians may provide. Historical explanations and their *explananda* are irreducibly heterogeneous. However a role of theory is to impose order on heterogeneity. To hold that history is presently conceived as a motley of past events, explained by any variety of causal or interpretive considerations, says nothing about historical materialism's prospects. It may be that there is no general theory of historical processes. But it may also be that the experienced complexity of the texture of history can give way to laws of its underlying dynamic. Neither claim is amenable to a priori proof or confutation. Whether or not history admits of a general theory is an issue to be discovered, not settled by fiat. Should historical materialism or some rival theory of comparable generality prove sustainable, the case against atheoreticism will be made. Meanwhile the issue remains open.

In any case, the outcome should not matter much for particular historical explanations. Despite what many Marxists suppose, a general theory of history like historical materialism is too coarse to affect particular explanations significantly. Thus history itself might follow a technological imperative, while particular events are explicable on quite different grounds. Practising historians, like evolutionary biologists are, in the main, micro-theorists. Historical materialists, on the other hand, are only macro-theorists, concerned with large-scale trends and epochal transformations. The principles that govern the macro-theory need not have explanatory resonance at the micro-level.

It is worth noting that, strictly speaking, historical materialism neither supports nor informs the view that there are general sociological laws adequate for explaining particular events, apart from its own laws, including its claims about the relation between base and superstructure. Historical materialist laws are general in scope, applicable wherever there is scarcity and wherever persons are sufficiently rational to want to ameliorate their condition and capable of doing so through technological development. Historical materialism is not, however, a general sociology: a set of trans-historical sociological laws. Indeed, by construing fundamental historical periods as natural kinds, analogous to elements in the periodic table, historical materialism suggests, without quite implying, that there are no general sociological laws of a sort that would interest practising historians. The implication, instead, is that beyond what is gained by situating an event in an historical epoch, what is important explanatorily will vary from epoch to epoch. In evolutionary theory, on the other hand, epochal divisions do not comprise distinct natural kinds but fortuitous confluences of causal factors. It would therefore be astonishing to find differences between evolutionary laws that apply in one period and laws that apply in another. Indeed, if Darwin was right, there are no differences of moment: natural selection is the principal evolutionary force throughout all of natural history.

Historical materialism, on the other hand, periodizes history into discrete modes of production that are conceived as natural kind divisions. It provides a list of natural kinds in much the way that chemistry provides a list of elements (the periodic table). Unlike chemistry, though, historical materialism also accounts for the list it provides by appeal to an inherent dynamic. Natural and human history are essentially dynamic. Accordingly, historical materialism is a theory not just of possible variations, but of historical change.

It is not particularly unusual to claim, as historical materialism does, that history admits of epochal divisions or even that the periodization historical materialism proposes is explanatory. Concepts of feudalism, capitalism, and socialism are widely held to have explanatory force and even to indicate real historical divisions. What is contentious is the claim that there is a theory of this structure and of its dynamic. Historical materialism's distinctive historicity resides in its insistence on this very contentious point.

Endogenous/Exogenous

Historical materialism resembles teleological philosophies of history in conceiving the processes that move history along as endogenous.[7] It is ever-changing relations (of correspondence and non-correspondence) between forces and relations of production that account for modes of production and their sequencing. Historical materialist development is internal to systems constituted by forces and relations of production.

Mainstream historiography acknowledges few, if any, endogenous processes and in any case assigns them no special explanatory importance. Evolutionary biology does recognize some causal factors internal to evolving populations, for example, random genetic drift. However, mutation and natural selection are exogenous; and, from a Darwinian perspective, it is these mechanisms that account overwhelmingly for differences in the reproductive success of organisms. In the Darwinian world picture, evolutionary change is not, for the most part, internally driven. Where natural selection is the principal factor governing organismic change, evolution is mainly a matter of fitting organisms to their environments.[8]

Historical materialism, in contrast, recognizes only

endogenous causes. It does not even provide a way to describe exogenous sources of change. Of course, it is consistent with what the theory claims that, as a matter of fact, exogenous factors not recognized by historical materialism have causal efficacy. But just as Darwinians acknowledge many possible causes of evolution while insisting that natural selection is by far the most important, historical materialists hold that, as a matter of fact, the dynamic processes historical materialism recognizes actually do account for epochal historical transformations. Thus historical materialism favours endogenous over exogenous causes twice over: its general laws acknowledge only endogenous processes, and its associated historical hypothesis asserts that these endogenous processes have played a crucially important role in determining the shape of history.

Historical materialism's distinctive historicity consists precisely in the role it accords endogenous processes. Admittedly, it is possible to discern a structure and direction to change on the view that what prompts transformations in human societies is exogenous to historical systems. It might be held, for instance, that human history is best explained by changes in climate or by epidemiological factors or by any number of other exogenous causes. These causes could effectively divide history into discrete natural kinds. And it is even possible to imagine a theoretical warrant for sequencing these natural kind divisions into a determinate trajectory. We need only suppose that the exogenous causes are somehow joined systematically, say, by means of a general theory of climatological change or of human diseases. Then historical change would be connected directly with systematic changes in the exogenous variable. However, a theory that invests the dynamic of change in exogenous variables would differ radically from historical materialism. If the exogenous variables change systematically, history would have a predictable trajectory. But it still would not have a direction in the sense historical materialism claims.[9] There would be no internal necessity to the sequencing of events. An account of historical change that recognizes mainly exogenous causes would therefore remain a theory of historical variation only. Historical development would be 'epiphenomenal' and always, in principle, reversible. Historical materialist development, however, is irreversible.

Besides providing a description of history's structure, accounting for that structure, and ordering its items chronologically, historical materialism accounts for its chronological ordering by reference to a process that is endogenous to the system the theory identifies as its proper domain. Without acceding to the teleological structure of earlier philosophies of history, historical materialism conceives change propelled along by an internal necessity. In this way, it retrieves the radical historicity of its philosophical predecessors, while respecting the conceptual structure and maintaining the explanatory objectives of modern scientific practice.

Weak and Weaker Historical Materialisms

We have seen that orthodox historical materialism provides an account (a) of necessary material conditions for change; (b) of the direction of change; (c) of the means through which change is achieved; and (d) of sufficient conditions for change. As already noted, the least plausible of these claims is (d). There is no good reason to assert that an interest in change suffices to bring about the requisite material, organizational, and intellectual capacities for change; and no reason, therefore, to propose an inevitable sequence of epochal historical stages.[10] What I shall call weak historical materialism, claiming just (a), (b) and (c), but not (d), therefore suggests itself.[11] Weak historical materialism is not trivial. It is a theory of what is and is not on the historical agenda for different levels of development of productive forces. It depicts a map of economic structures — an account of the pattern of 'junctures' (relations of correspondence or 'contradiction' between forces and relations of production) — and accounts, as well, for the direction of movement along the map. In addition, weak historical materialism advances a substantive claim about the means by which historical change and stasis is achieved. It is class struggle that accounts for movement along the map the theory provides. Weak historical materialism, in short, is the orthodox theory without the unlikely and unwarranted claim that what is necessary for epochal historical change is ultimately also sufficient.

The orthodox theory claims that whenever epochal historical change comes to accord with the general, trans-historical human interest in augmenting the rate of development of productive forces, eventually that change will occur — subject only to the obvious provisos that conditions for sustaining human life remain in effect and that the conditions under which the theory applies i.e. relative scarcity and the rationality of persons — continue to pertain. Where an interest in change exists, the capacities for change follow inevitably. Weak historical materialism is more circumspect. Change is not claimed to follow directly from an interest in change; the capacity for change is a non-redundant second ingredient that must also be present. But both orthodox and weak historical materialism hold that there is a lawlike tendency for relations of production to correspond to forces of production in order to facilitate the continuous development of productive forces. Orthodox and weak historical materialism differ in their purported explanatory force, but they acknowledge the same internal dynamic and are therefore historical theories in the same way.

A theory of history that advanced only (a) and (b) — what might be called quasi-historical materialism — is also conceivable. In order to deny (c) plausibly, quasi-historical materialism would have to propose an alternative, non-Marxian account of the means through which the pattern and direction it shares with weak and orthodox historical materialism is achieved. It is difficult to imagine what besides class struggle could have the effect of periodizing history into discrete modes of production (forms of control over the economic surplus and, therefore, of class domination), though perhaps not impossible to do so. Independently developing political institutions could play this role.[12] Needless to say, quasi-historical materialism diverges substantively from the letter and spirit of Marx's theory of history. In denying a fundamental role to class struggle, it is a non-Marxian historical materialism. However, so long as the driving mechanism of change is considered internal to historical systems, quasi-historical materialism would still be historical in just the way the orthodox theory is.

There are even more radical retreats from the explanatory pretensions of the orthodox theory that, however, are still Marxian in privileging class struggle; retreats involving mitigations of the generality of the orthodox theory. These restricted historical materialisms bear mention both because they may prove more sustainable than weak historical materialism and because it is instructive to appreciate how far one can stray from the letter of the orthodox theory without undoing its distinctive historicity. Weak, like orthodox, historical materialism purports to be a general theory of history and also a fundamental or primary theory, a theory of general history, that is, of legal and juridical superstructures and also of 'forms of consciousness'. The theory aims, in other words, to account for large-scale features of history's structure and trajectory but also to reveal historical processes that are fundamental for explaining the rest of human history. It is far from obvious though that history admits of a general theory in the way historical materialists have supposed; and still less obvious that historical materialism is a theory of general history.

It might be held, for instance, that the theory pertains not to all of human history nor even just to the history of class societies, as *The Communist Manifesto* suggests, but only to the history of certain kinds of class societies. A natural way to construe this proposed restriction on the generality of the theory is as an historical hypothesis. Then the position would be that historical materialist development was, as a matter of fact, overwhelmed by rival causes — perhaps of an exogenous character — for some, but not all of human history. Or it might be claimed that the theory, even in principle, applies only to certain parts of human history. Marx plainly did accord considerable generality to the theory he proposed; and it would remain to provide an alternative rationale, distinct from the indications Marx provided, for limiting historical materialism's purported generality. Still, a weak historical materialism — satisfying (a), (b) and (c) — but applying to less of human history than Marx intended is conceivable. Such a theory would be no less historical than historical materialisms of more general explanatory pretensions.

Historical materialism might also be modified by mitigating its claims to be a theory of general history. It could be held, for instance, that only certain aspects of history can be theorized in the way historical materialism supposes; that historical materialism is only a theory of economic structures and therefore of legal and juridical superstructures and ideologies only insofar as they affect economic structures.[13] This retreat from orthodoxy would, of course, diminish historical materialism's role as a primary or fundamental theory but, again, it would not detract from its historicity.

In sum, the putative generality of the theory does not matter at all for its historicity. Should it turn out, after proper consideration, that a defensible historical materialism pertains to much less of history than its proponents have thought or explains much less than has been claimed, historical materialism would be a less ambitious theory than Marx intended, but not a less historical theory.

Care must be exercised, though, in distinguishing properly historical materialist positions, however weakened or mitigated, from positions that part ways with the distinctive core of Marx's theory. It is particularly important to take care when genuinely alternative positions are propounded in a still Marxian framework and even in an historical materialist idiom. Thus some Marxists have advanced a view of historical materialism as a theory of social forms, but not of the transitions between these forms.[14] Then historical materialism would become a materialist sociology; a set of laws that purport to explain by means of materialist categories.[15] But a materialist sociology is not a materialist theory of history. Purported historical materialisms that do not theorize transitions, that fail to postulate a direction of change between epochal structures, are not versions of historical materialism in the sense in question here. They are not even historical theories in the much more limited respect in which Darwinian evolutionary theory is historical.

Can We Be Confident in the Theory?

Just as there is no a priori defence to be provided for historical materialism's general laws or for the associated historical hypothesis that these laws in fact apply, there is no a priori way to adjudicate between the rival historical materialisms sketched in the preceding section. Ultimately, historical evidence will be decisive. In this respect too, historical materialism is like any theory that purports to explain phenomena by discovering their causal determinations. However historical materialist claims are not liable to immediate corroboration or refutation. Marx's theory is more like a research agenda or paradigm than a set of verifiable hypotheses; and it is only very recently that the theory has been reconstructed with sufficient clarity that its merits can begin to be constructively assessed. At this point, it is not yet entirely clear what would count as corroborating or refuting evidence. In the end, empirical considerations do bear decisively on the theory's acceptability. But it is unlikely, even discounting ideological interferences and other obstacles in the path of rational adjudication, that the issue will be settled incontrovertibly in the foreseeable future.

I have suggested that orthodox historical materialism is almost certainly not sustainable and I have registered, in passing, some doubts about historical materialism's claims to be a general and primary theory of history. These suggestions, however, should be read as barely elaborated intuitions about what the pertinent evidence supports. It is possible, at this degree of remove from historical research, to demonstrate historical materialism's cogency and to suggest its plausibility by appealing to widely held beliefs about history. These considerations fall short, however, of a full-scale defence of the Marxian theory of history in any of its conceivable variations. In the best of circumstances, the case for or against historical materialism must be developed over time by many investigators. A clear account of the theory's conceptual structure and distinctive historicity is only a preliminary step in this enormous undertaking.

Whatever the truth turns out to be, it is plain already that we can be more confident in weak than orthodox historical materialism and, particularly, in versions of weak historical materialism that minimize its claims to be a general and primary theory. Should the more ambitious claims proferred by orthodox Marxists be sustained, these weaker claims would follow in turn. If orthodoxy cannot be born out, the weaker versions of the theory still stand a good chance of capturing and explaining the fundamental characteristics of human history. Fortunately, for joining historical materialism with Rousseauean political philosophy, it is not necessary to advert to orthodoxy nor to suppose that historical materialism is a general and primary theory in the way Marxists have commonly supposed. A weak historical materialism that applies in principle just to capitalism and socialism will suffice. And it will be enough if the theory accounts for superstructural aspects of social formations only insofar as they figure in the reproduction and transformation of these modes of production.

By focusing on the distinctive historicity of historical materialism, I have not tried to defend the theory. I have, though, exhibited its internal cogency and, in doing so, provided some basis for confidence in it. The political theory I shall go on to develop will suppose that a weak and attenuated historical materialism ultimately *can* be sustained. On that plausible but still contestable assumption, elements of Rousseauean political philosophy can be set free from their utopian carapace and put to work in defence of the end of the state.

6
Socialism

This chapter investigates socialism in view of Marx's theory of history. An account of socialism, its varieties and its possible futures will be indispensable for joining the core insights of historical materialism with elements of the political theory developed by Rousseau and his critics, both revolutionary and conservative, and with other aspects of Marx's theory of the state and revolution.

Socialism in Historical Materialism

For all varieties of historical materialism, what propels epochal historical change is a universal and trans-historical human interest in developing the forces of production. Insofar as individuals can adapt means to ends, this interest will have historical effects, and there will be a tendency for forces of production to develop. But development renders economic structures unstable. Contradictions between forces and relations of production emerge, and since the tendency for forces of production to develop is inexorable, contradictions will be resolved in favour of the productive forces. Production relations that have come to fetter development will be transformed into production relations that facilitate development. Thus the continuous development of forces of production, taken as a transhistorical imperative, elicits radical discontinuities in social relations of production or, what comes to the same thing, revolutionary transformations of economic structures.

So long as it is not blocked by rival forces, historical materialist development terminates when contradictions cease or, equivalently, when permanent structural compatability between forces and relations of production is achieved. In principle, this result might be achieved in either of two ways. An economic structure capable of developing productive forces indefinitely might, at some point, emerge and remain in place permanently, free from endogenous pressures for change. Or else, in consequence of the massive development of productive forces, scarcity might cease to pervade the human condition and shape human interests. Then we could expect the dimunition and eventually the demise of the developmental imperative that, in the historical materialist view, had to that point structured the course of human history. Orthodox historical materialism avers the latter alternative. Capitalism, which might appear capable of guaranteeing continuous development, is held incapable of reproducing itself indefinitely. But once productive forces are sufficiently developed — first under capitalism, then, after capitalism's collapse, under socialism — there will be a massive economic surplus. Human interests will be radically transformed, and development will lose its potency as an historical force. Class society itself will become a fetter on the rational deployment of productive capacities. Historical materialist development will therefore wither away for want of a *raison d'être.* Communism, a classless society founded on material abundance, will supersede class societies. The end of historical materialist development will finally be reached. Of course, even under communism, development might still be a chosen course. Communist development, however, would no longer be a blind imperative of the economic system but a matter of deliberate collective choice.

Since, in the orthodox view, an interest in epochal change is sufficient for bringing epochal change about, communism is the inevitable consequence of the contradictions of class society. Weak historical materialism, however, regards interests and capacities for change as independent and, therefore, denies communism's inevitability, even in the long run. Communism is only possible, not necessary. Historical materialist development creates material conditions for communism, but nothing more. Weak historical materialism does not quite predict the end of historical materialist development but provides, instead, an account of material conditions for the possibility of its demise. How this possibility might be actualized falls beyond the purview of the theory.

Inasmuch as weak historical materialism is by far the more plausible variant of the theory, what follows here addresses the question of the future of class society from its perspective. This perspective makes the historical materialist map more complex than Marxians have traditionally assumed. If the epochal transformations that give structure and direction to history are only possible, not necessary, there can be historical outcomes other than the inevitable communist future proclaimed by Marx. Still socialism will designate a natural kind division, the historical successor of capitalism. And socialism will remain the final epochal structure. For all historical materialisms, communism does not come about through an epochal transformation in the way that capitalism and socialism do. Indeed, communism is not strictly an economic structure at all. It is the termination of socialism, the limiting case, the end of the entire process historical materialism aims to recount and explain.

Marxists have traditionally accepted these beliefs uncritically. It is well, though, that they be examined carefully, for neither the integrity of socialism as an epochal historical division nor its connection with communism are as sure as Marxists have traditionally maintained. Nevertheless, despite serious flaws in the traditional view, these claims are finally defensible.

Socialism As Post-Capitalism

Once orthodoxy is abandoned, its prediction of capitalism's inevitable demise must be abandoned too. Weak historical materialism, if true, shows only that capitalism need not continue indefinitely, not that it cannot. If capacities for change are irreducible to interests in change, development by itself will be insufficient for engendering capacities for further development. Indeed, it is sometimes held that development under capitalism decapacitates the proletariat as an agent of revolutionary change. Thus it is argued that consumerism i.e. the augmentation of effective demand by policies supporting high levels of consumption, brings about the integration of the working class into the existing order, deflecting its revolutionary potential. Or it is suggested that the internationalization of capital and the resulting segmentation of the work force involved in the production process in world industries undoes the organizational capacities of workers. Insofar as these or other characteristics of capitalist society are consequences of internal developmental imperatives, capitalist development would actually block its own demise and transformation. It is conceivable, in other words, that capitalism might prevail indefinitely not in spite of but because of development, whether or not its continuation somehow comes to fetter further development. This possibility is strictly consistent with weak historical materialist positions.

There is, however, an aspect of the orthodox notion of an inevitable sequencing of economic structures that weak historical materialism retains: the claim that forces of production develop continuously and irreversibly. Then transformations in economic structures, when they occur, track ever-increasing levels of development. In this sense, epochal change is always progressive. When change occurs it is to accommodate the fundamental human interest in augmenting the level of development of productive forces.

Since social relations of production are conceived as real (not merely juridical) property relations, we can grasp what is progressive in the transition from one set of production relations to another by focusing on changes in real property relations as societies proceed along the historical materialist map. With this focus, we can discern yet another sense in which historical materialism's sequencing of economic structures is progressive.

Before capitalism, private property existed not only in physical assets employed in the production process, but also in direct producers. There was property in persons. This form of real property existed in varying forms. In what Marx called the 'ancient mode of production' and in other slave societies, some individuals held rights over others similar to those commonly enjoyed over land, tools and animals. Indeed, in some instances, masters' rights over slaves exceeded their rights over other productive assets, since slaves could usually be bought and sold while land, the principal non-human productive asset, often could not. At the other extreme were the more mitigated forms of ownership of persons characteristic, for instance, of late feudalism in Europe.[1] With the transition to capitalism, ownership of direct producers ended; except in the sense that everyone owns his or her own person.[2] Under capitalism, there are no economically significant juridical or customary relations of bondage or hierarchy. But there is still private ownership of society's principal, non-human means of production.

Socialism will be understood here to designate any political economic arrangement that can succeed capitalism, according to the historical materialist map of possibilities. By socialism, then, I mean post-capitalism. Socialism carries the deprivatization of productive assets a step beyond capitalism. In addition to deprivatizing ownership of persons, it deprivatizes ownership of society's non-human means of production — the alienable, material assets used in the production process.

This understanding of socialism is weaker and more inclusive than Marx's. The definition does not address the issue of class structure. In particular, it does not require that, under socialism, the working class be the ruling class. And it does not incorporate the political objectives that motivate most socialists. Socialists, Marxian and non-Marxian alike, characteristically intend a good deal more than the elimination of private property in alienable, non-human means of production. Socialists want, among other things, the radical democratization of economic life, the end of war and international animosities, the mitigation of racial, ethnic and sexual oppression, and the advance of material equality. But these hopes and expectations do not figure in the definition proposed here. Indeed, it is not immediately evident why the end of private property in alienable means of production is desirable at all. The definition offered here is apt, however, for depicting socialism from the perspective provided by Marx's theory of history. It is also apt insofar as it instructive to distinguish what socialists hope to achieve under socialism from socialism itself.[3]

To characterize the succession of economic structures from precapitalist class societies to capitalism to post-capitalist or socialist societies by reference to the progressive deprivatization of property relations in means of production — eliminating, first, private ownership of persons and, then, private ownership of alienable, non-human productive assets — is tantamount to describing epochal historical change as the progressive elimination of forms of exploitation. Exploitation will be understood here as a process for generating material inequalities, based upon prior inequalities in the distribution of power. Where exploitation exists, there is an exploited party who could do better (materially), but for the exploiting party who actually does do better at the exploited party's expense. In the Marxian view, the differential power relations that generate material inequalities are always property relations — systems of rules regulating individuals' control over productive assets. The location of the pertinent differential power relations in systems of property is the core idea — and distinctive feature — of the Marxian view of exploitation.

Marx's own account of exploitation stressed the coercive aspect of exploitation relations.[4] The emphasis here, however, will be on exploitation's distributive implications. This emphasis is appropriate insofar as the intent is to join exploitation theory with historical materialism. However it is incomplete. Exploitation is an evil not just because of its distributive effects, but because these effects are achieved through force.[5] Were this the place to analyse exploitation and justify the intuition that it is an evil to be avoided, the coercive aspects of exploitation relations would have to be addressed. However it is not necessary to analyse exploitation fully to profit from the concept's usefulness for identifying real historical divisions. In what follows, I therefore accede to intuition and assume without further argument that exploitation is indeed an evil. If this assumption is right, the successive elimination of forms of exploitation is progressive not only indirectly — for tracking ever-higher levels of development of productive forces — but also for its own sake provided, of course, total exploitation actually decreases when a form of exploitation is removed. That is, provided new forms of exploitation do not arise or remaining forms intensify enough to counter the gain.

It should be noted too that social relations can be exploitative, in the ordinary sense of the term, without generating material inequalities and that these non-economic forms of exploitation are ignored in the definition I have proposed. Non-economic exploitation is admittedly of considerable importance in current political discussion and theoretical debate, including debates internal to Marxism. But it is only economic exploitation that is pertinent to historical materialism's periodization of history and its account of history's direction. Non-economic exploitation will therefore be overlooked here.

It is now clear that Marx conceived exploitation inadequately and only for special cases.[6] Marx's interest, overwhelmingly, was in capitalist exploitation, perhaps because he believed that the elimination of exploitation under capitalism was tantamount to the elimination of exploitation as such. However, even for Marx, capitalist exploitation is not the only form exploitation can take. There is also feudal exploitation. In Europe and elsewhere, before the elimination of property in persons, serfs were obliged to work a fixed time for the benefit of their lords; or else they were obliged to provide their lords with a portion of the product of their labour. In this way, material inequalities were generated in consequence of differential ownership of productive assets. In conceiving capitalist exploitation as the appropriation by capitalists of the 'surplus value' workers produce, Marx sought to show — with the conceptual apparatus of classical economic theory — that exploitation can survive the elimination of private property in persons. Exploitation, then, was already a concept of some generality for Marx, admitting at least two forms. The project of generalizing the concept further, of showing how exploitation persists under a variety of changes in real property relations, has lately been carried out by John Roemer.[7] It is therefore possible, following Roemer, to exhibit exploitation's different forms more completely than traditional Marxism attempted.

Among the conceptual strategies Roemer employs to conceptualize exploitation is a 'game' theoretic approach that is useful for characterizing exploitation's distinct, historically pertinent forms.[8] Following Roemer, we can conceive of a political economic system as a 'game' in which the economic agents are players. A group of individuals, a coalition, is exploited in some game if there are withdrawal rules under which that coalition could command more resources by not playing the game than by continuing to play, and under which another coalition, its complement, would be worse off in virtue of the withdrawal of the exploited coalition. Then those who could do better are exploited and those who benefit from their exploitation are exploiters.

Thus, under feudalism, serfs worked their own property some days and their lord's property other days. Or they worked a single piece of land, but gave over some of the produce of their labour to their lord. If the serfs had withdrawn from this arrangement, taking the land they worked and their other means of production with them, they would have been better off, for they could then retain the entire product of their labour.

Correspondingly, the lords would have been worse off. Then the lords benefited at the serfs' expense in virtue of the rules of the (feudal) game; the serfs were exploited and the lords were their exploiters. Feudal exploitation exists, then, whenever there are individuals who could do better if they withdrew from the feudal economy with their personal assets. If we suppose what sometimes was not the case — that serfs owned their means of production (the family plot and the tools and animals with which the family plot was worked) — we can say that feudal exploitation exists wherever there is a coalition that would be materially better off if it withdrew with its private property in alienable means of production. The imagined withdrawal is tantamount, of course, to replacing feudalism with capitalism.

It might have been, however, that despite appropriating the surplus product made by serfs, feudal lords provided indispensable services. Perhaps they provided military protection or organized manor life. Then it could be argued that feudal exploitation in fact did not exist, because the exchanges serfs were obliged to make in view of prevailing property relations were not in fact to their detriment. This rejoinder is surely unsustainable on any reasonable assessment of the facts. But the claim is conceptually apt. For exploitation to exist, the putatively exploited party must do worse than it otherwise might in consequence of the rules of the game it is obliged to play.

Roemer then holds that capitalist exploitation exists if there are withdrawal rules under which a coalition would do better if it withdrew from the game defined by capitalist property relations, and its complement would do worse. Were proletarians, direct producers not owning their means of production, to withdraw from the capitalist economy according to the withdrawal rule proposed for feudal exploitation — were they to withdraw with their alienable, productive assets — they plainly would not be better off. For then the only productive asset each member of this coalition possesses, the capacity to labour, would be rendered unusable. Given capitalist property relations, the exchange of labour power for a wage plainly is advantageous, even for proletarians. But it does not then follow that capitalist exploitation does not exist. For the question is not whether, under capitalism, the wage bargain is advantageous for the proletariat (plainly it is); but whether capitalism itself is.

Thus Roemer asks whether there are individuals who would do better were they to withdraw from the capitalist game taking with them not only their privately owned assets, but also their per capita share of society's alienable assets. The answer, he argues, is yes — for those who, in consequence of capitalist property relations, are obliged to sell their labour power for a wage. Were alienable assets deprivatized, the proletariat would be better off. Therefore capitalist exploitation does exist; provided, again, that capitalists do not perform indispensable functions (like organizing the production process or bearing risks) that render the wage bargain advantageous even for the putatively exploited coalition. In consequence of the system of private property that defines capitalism, owners of capital exploit non-owners (proletarians), the direct producers whose labour power is set to work on the means of production capitalists own.

Socialism may then be defined as an economic system without feudal and capitalist exploitation, that is, without the forms of exploitation Marx imagined. It does not therefore follow that socialism is a society without exploitation. Traditionally, Marxists have not had much to say about exploitation under socialism, not because historical materialism excludes the possibility — quite the contrary — but because Marxism has been joined historically with a political vision that focused attention on the evils of capitalism and the advantages of socialism, to the exclusion of concern over evils that might survive or be exacerbated in post-capitalist societies. But this optimism, however natural and expedient, is naive. It is also remediable. And a remedy is plainly called for in view of the evident distance separating existing socialism from the socialism Marx envisaged and from communism.

Exploitation Under Socialism

Anti-feudal revolutionaries believed that the elimination of feudal exploitation would usher in, if not heaven on earth, then as close an approximation as earthly beings can reasonably hope to achieve. By the mid-nineteenth century, these expectations proved manifestly false. Of course, the replacement of feudalism by capitalism was still hailed as progressive, not just for reasons historical materialism acknowledges, but also according to the vaguer intuitions we all share. However the end of feudalism was not sufficient for fulfilling the aspirations of anti-feudal revolutionaries. Liberty, equality and fraternity remained goals, but the transition from feudalism to capitalism was increasingly seen as necessary but not sufficient for their realization. Many progressive thinkers in the early nineteenth century even came to regard these goals as insufficient.

Marx's demonstration of the continuation of exploitation under capitalism — in a new and less transparent form — explains, in part, the failed hopes of anti-feudal revolutionaries.[9] Contrary to what had been supposed, the end of ownership of persons did not end exploitation. Instead, exploitation survived the transition from coerced to 'free' labour markets. Insofar as exploitation is an evil, its continuation in a new form is a reason why feudalism's demise did not fulfil the expectations of anti-feudal revolutionaries. It is also a reason, among others, why feudalism's historical successor must itself be put in question. In showing that the core idea, though not the institutional form, of feudal exploitation survived the transition from feudalism to capitalism, Marx put the moral status of capitalism in question.[10]

Anti-capitalist revolutionaries, including Marx, now appear, like their anti-feudal predecessors, to have been naïve in their estimation of the consequences of eliminating capitalist exploitation. It is plain that existing socialism has not ushered in even a remote approximation of heaven on earth, despite the expectations and sacrifices of so many. To note this unhappy fact is not to deny the historical advance even existing socialism registers over capitalism, any more than recognition of capitalism's shortcomings implies a denial of capitalism's historical advance over feudalism. But it does call attention to the need to investigate forms of exploitation that survive the deprivatization of ownership of alienable means of production.

That exploitation survives the move beyond capitalism is clear from historical materialism's view of history's structure and direction. Therefore Marxists' characteristic disregard of exploitation under socialism cannot be blamed on the Marxian theory of history. Just as the end of feudalism eliminated only feudal exploitation, not exploitation as such, the end of capitalism eliminates only capitalist exploitation, leaving remaining forms of exploitation in place and perhaps even expanding their scope and force. The investigation of exploitation under capitalism is useful for focusing attention on one of capitalism's evils and, more importantly, for providing insight into capitalism's future. Similarly, an account of exploitation under socialism will identify some of the evils that remain after capitalism has passed and help too in speculating on the possible futures of socialism.

In the classical formulation, under socialism ('the first phase of communism'), income and other societal benefits are distributed according to productive contribution. 'The right of the producers,' Marx and Engels declare, 'is to be *proportional* to the labour they supply.'[11] This principle is sometimes thought to govern distributions under capitalism also. But productive contributions under socialism are ascertained through an 'equal standard', labour time; a standard that effectively precludes capitalists' profits. Socialism and capitalism therefore do not quite suppose the same principle. However, it is only with the economic and moral evolution to communism that the 'horizons of bourgeois right' can be finally transcended. 'After the productive forces have also increased with the all-round development of the individual, and all the springs of cooperative wealth flow more abundantly — only then can the narrow horizon of bourgeois right be crossed in its entirety and society inscribe on its banners: From each according to his ability, to each according to his needs!'[12]

For Marx, then, differential returns proportional to differential productive contributions continue under socialism in its first stages, as a concession to the legacy of history. The not yet attainable ideal is to transcend 'bourgeois right'. It should be noted, though, that not all differential returns based on labour time enjoy the same moral status. Those that result from different expenditures of effort (because some individuals work longer or more intensely than others) seem entirely fair; provided effort is expended in consequence of genuinely autonomous choice. Arguably, it is also fair for different skill levels to be rewarded differentially as compensation for the costs of acquiring skills, so long as no 'monopoly rent' is charged in addition. These cases should be distinguished from instances where individuals produce differentially because they work with different technologies, or where they have different skills. Then neither free choice nor fair compensation accounts, in the main, for differences in outcomes.[13]

The case where workers are supplied with different technologies is impossible to evaluate in general. The fact that workers in one sector are supplied with means of production that augment their level of productivity beyond the level of workers in another sector conveys no justification by itself for differential rewards. It matters how the more productive workers came to be supplied with superior means of production. Did the differences across sectors arise in ways that generate legitimate claims on societal benefits? If not, the presumption in favour of egalitarian distribution would carry, excluding considerations of efficiency. In actual cases, the situation will probably not admit of easy assessment. What is clear is that differential productivity by itself — unlike differential effort — does not suffice to warrant unequal returns.[14]

'To each according to productive contribution' is, it seems, an amalgam of distributivist and welfarist considerations. In cases of differential effort, unequal rewards are warranted by considerations of justice. In other cases, unequal rewards, proportional to productivity, are concessions to the need, encouraged under capitalism, to allocate and motivate producers by recourse to material incentives. Arguably, this need will always offend justice, but the extent of the offence will vary.[15] Where different levels of productivity result from different provisions of means of production, the moral assessment of the outcome will depend on how the unequal provision came about. Where different levels of productivity result from different distributions of skills, similar considerations apply. Insofar as skills are acquired (or developed) through effort, it does seem fair to reward their deployment differentially. But insofar as skills are innate, their distribution is morally arbitrary. Differential rewards based on their exercise are therefore unjust, whether or not they are necessary for welfarist reasons. In both cases, though, the more skilled have power over the less skilled in virtue of the control they exercise over skills, a productive asset that is 'inalienable' from their persons. They are therefore able to demand income at the expense of the less skilled in exchange for the deployment of this resource. They are, in a word, exploiters.

Roemer calls this form of exploitation 'socialist exploitation'. Socialist (or, better, skills) exploitation, like feudal and capitalist exploitation, may be conceived in 'game' theoretic fashion. 'A coalition is socialistically exploited if it could improve its lot by withdrawing with its per capita share of society's inalienable assets, once alienable assets are distributed equally.'[16] Marx and Engels believed that the practice of rewarding skills differentially is unavoidable before communism; that it cannot be eliminated without giving rise to debilitating incentive problems, perhaps even eliminating the skills that provide the basis for high levels of productivity and therefore for socialism itself. Thus they prescribed the continuation of skills exploitation in the first stages of socialism. The moral fact remains however: that skills exploitation is a form of exploitation, that it generally offends justice and that, insofar as society can bear the cost of its elimination, it ought to be eliminated.

In existing (and likely) socialist countries, inequalities are generated by skills exploitation, but it is plain that another form of exploitation, 'status exploitation' in Roemer's terminology, is bound to be of far greater importance. Status exploitation exists when inequalities arise out of incumbency of positions in hierarchically structured organizations. In other words, when there is a coalition of individuals who would do better, and a complementary coalition who would do worse, without differential returns based on positions. Status exploitation may be indispensable under socialism, at least initially, just as skills exploitation apparently is. It is certainly pervasive in existing socialism. However, it too is a form of exploitation that, like skills exploitation, ought, wherever feasible, to be eliminated.

The term 'status exploitation' is unfortunate, since all exploitation is in some sense a consequence of status. With feudal, capitalist and skills exploitation, differential status is transparently a consequence of control over productive resources — in persons, in non-human alienable assets and in inalienable assets, respectively. Status exploitation too is a consequence of 'ownership' of productive assets, though less transparently so. The special privileges and material advantages enjoyed by incumbents of high party, military and bureaucratic positions in existing socialist countries result from effective control (real ownership) over administrative and organizational resources. It is the command structure that directs the production process in existing socialist countries, not just at the level of the individual enterprise but at the societal level as well, that is the basis for status or, more appropriately, organizational, exploitation.[17]

Skills and organizational exploitation, then, are the characteristic forms of exploitation in socialist societies. Each exists, of course, under capitalism as well; though, under capitalism, they are not nearly so consequential as capitalist exploitation itself. In general, movement along the historical materialist map involves the successive elimination of forms of exploitation. Thus in pre-capitalist societies inequalities can be generated by four distinct forms of exploitation — based on control over persons, over alienable means of production, and over skills and organizational resources — though, in fact, only ownership of persons is likely to be significant. Capitalist societies, in turn, admit capitalist, skills and organizational exploitation — with capitalist exploitation generally predominant. Socialist societies allow only skills and organizational exploitation. The elimination of a form of exploitation in each case is progressive but, again, it does not insure that aggregate exploitation diminishes. Remaining forms of exploitation can expand to fill the void left by the elimination of the form of exploitation principally responsible for generating inequalities under its historical predecessor. Existing socialist societies appear to suffer acutely from this phenomenon, among others.

Exploitation and the State

The transition from socialism to communism has never been easy to comprehend in Marxian terms. But the identification of forms of exploitation that survive the transition from capitalism to socialism makes the transition to communism even more problematic than would otherwise be thought. For Marx, the exploiting class in an economic structure is always a ruling class, it organizes and reproduces its domination of subordinate classes politically. If exploitation continues under socialism, then under socialism there should be a tendency, as in pre-socialist societies, for the principal exploiting class to use political power to organize and reproduce its dominant position. So, far from expecting the socialist state to wither away in accord with Marx's prediction, we should expect the consolidation and continuation of the state and the perpetuation indefinitely — by political means — of the forms of exploitation socialism supports. If socialism is indeed the final epochal historical division, this situation should continue indefinitely. It would then follow that socialism cannot result in communism.

Marxists have avoided drawing this conclusion by supposing that the ruling class under socialism is always the working class, the principal exploited class under capitalism. The working class, it is held, has no 'objective interest' in the continuation of its own position as a class. Then to the degree exploitation ceases to facilitate the expansion of productive forces, direct producers will have an interest in the elimination of exploitation as such. That the working class has an interest in ending capitalist exploitation is clear. Arguably, workers also have an interest in eliminating forms of exploitation that survive the end of capitalism. Incumbents of commanding positions in the economy and the state, like capitalists, benefit at the expense of direct producers. Thus the working class is a victim of organizational exploitation and has an interest in its termination. There is also an interest in ending skills exploitation, at least on the part of workers, assumed to be the vast majority, who are not in a position to exploit skills acquired in the 'natural lottery'. The working class can therefore be expected to use state power to obliterate both the residuals of capitalist exploitation and also the forms of exploitation likely to afflict post-capitalist societies.

However this conclusion is at odds not only with the evidence of existing socialism, but also with the claim, canonical in the Marxian tradition since *The Communist Manifesto*, that the principal exploiting class is always a ruling class. By supposing political power under socialism to be in the hands of the workers, Marxists, in effect, deny this central Marxian thesis. For if the working class holds political power, the principal exploiting class is not, in fact, a ruling class. Instead, the exploiters are dominated politically by the class they exploit. Marxists characteristically overlook this embarrassing opposition between political theory and political conviction, in part because of allegiance to historical materialist orthodoxy and its prediction of communism's inevitability, but also because of a failure to acknowledge the full generality of the Marxian concept of exploitation and, therefore, the persistence of exploitation under socialism. We have seen, however, that claims for communism's inevitability almost certainly cannot be sustained and that exploitation does survive the transition from capitalism to socialism. That there is indeed a 'socialist road' to communism is therefore very much in need of demonstration.

I will argue in chapters 7 and 8 that socialism can result in communism. But first it will be well to investigate a related position Marx certainly also believed: the claim that *only* socialism can result in communism. The idea that there might be a non-socialist road to communism seems perverse. It is also, finally, unsustainable. Yet it is not so obviously wrong as may appear. It is a possibility worth taking seriously in its own right and worth considering too in order to focus on the role of the state in the transformation to communism.

Socialism and Communism

By defining communism as socialism's 'final phase', classical Marxism effectively foreclosed debate on the necessity of socialism for communism. This definition even suggests that communism, not socialism, is the alternative to capitalism; that socialism is only a transitional period for weeding out capitalist ways and establishing genuinely communist social relations.[18] However this formulation confounds political objectives with theoretical commitments, to the detriment of both. It is best, therefore, to rely on the historical materialist account and acknowledge socialism as capitalism's historical alternative and successor. Communism, then, is a form of socialism. As noted, historical materialism by itself does not suggest that this form will evolve out of socialism's initial stages. Quite the contrary. Even if it is conceded, in deference to orthodoxy, that socialism is inevitable, communism would still remain problematic.

Historical materialism provides a periodization of history according to which communism is an intra-epochal variation. However historical materialism is not all of Marxism. It is a theory that aims only to account for history's structure and direction. There is no reason why a theory with this explanatory objective should propose natural kind divisions that accord with what matters most to Marxian politics or the fundamental, human aspirations that motivate it. Thus, for Marx, historical materialism's periodization of history pales before another, deeper periodization: the division between pre-communist societies, including non-communist socialisms, and communism. From this perspective, the advent of communism marks the dawn of a new era.

Marx was loath to speculate on the character of communist society, in part to differentiate his views from those of 'utopian socialists', in part because it seemed pointless to prophesy a future that could be only dimly perceived. When Marx broached the idea of communism, it was usually in passing and in terms that evoke the moral vision we know from *The Social Contract.* Thus we are told that communism is 'the realm of freedom', the termination and culmination of 'the realm of necessity' in which humanity has toiled throughout all of history. It is implied too that communism has momentous and positive implications for a host of other values from justice to community and, above all, that communism advances the human capacity for self-realization. As Rousseau claimed for the *de jure* state,[19] the human prospect is enhanced enormously by the leap from 'necessity' to 'freedom'.

This formulation suggests the vision sketched by Marx in the 1844 *Economic and Philosophic Manuscripts* and throughout his early writings.[20] The main concern of these texts is the end of 'alienation', the separation of Man from His Essence, in the special, anthropological sense elaborated by Feuerbach and other Left Hegelians of the 1830s and 1840s. At stake ultimately, though, is autonomy.[21] In Marx's view, emancipation from 'alienated labour' is necessary and sufficient for achieving freedom in the sense that mattered for Rousseau and Kant. Labour, of course, continues in the ideal, communist order; no society can subsist without it. But the labour expended under communism is free labour, undertaken autonomously — a direct expression, Marx thought, of each producer's essential humanity.[22]

It is neither necessary nor feasible here to discuss the much-debated question of the role of 'alienation' in Marx's thought or the related issue of the connection between Marx's early and later writings. It will suffice to note that by the mid-1840s Marx had largely abandoned the philosophical anthropology that motivated his earlier invocation of 'essences' and their intra-subjective 'alienation'.[23] But the ideal of self-directed labour remained. Marx always conceived communism as a social order constituted by autonomous, productive activity; where labour is uncoerced but also, so far as possible, unconditioned by institutional circumstances.

Capitalist societies too have voluntary labour markets. In Marx's view then, free (autonomously determined) labour is not realized simply by eliminating outright coercion in the deployment of labour inputs to the production process. Like exploitation, 'alienated' (unfree) labour survives the transition from feudalism to capitalism, from authoritative labour allocations to voluntary labour markets. What rendered direct producers unfree in pre-capitalist societies was overt coercion. What renders workers unfree under capitalism is not overt. However the difference, in Marx's view, is at the level of appearance only.

So long as exploitation exists — so long as inequalities are generated in consequence of differential power relations (following from prevailing systems of ownership of productive assets) — labour is not fully free. Indeed, a central contention of the *Economic and Philosophic Manuscripts*, the essays *On the Jewish Question, The Critique of Hegel's Philosophy of Right* and many other early writings of Marx's is precisely that the transition to free wage labour masks an intensification of alienation, an exacerbation of 'unfreedom'.

The widespread intuition that market transactions generally — and therefore labour market exchanges — preserve freedom derives, in part, from attention to examples that plausibly do instance autonomous choice. When, in Adam Smith's 'early and rude state of society' (or Rousseau's ideal, yeoman polity), self-sufficient farmers exchange corn for wheat, the parties act autonomously. Since, by hypothesis, the parties to the exchange are largely self-sufficient, the transaction is not motivated by need but by a virtually unconditioned propensity 'to truck, barter and exchange'. To be sure, the farmers' respective situations help shape the preferences that motivate the transaction. It should even be possible in principle to provide a full causal account of the preference structures of the transacting parties and of their market behaviour. Unless causal determination itself is opposed to free choice, however, a causal account would not be likely to reveal anything that would count as freedom-restricting. The imagined exchange is voluntary but also autonomously undertaken. It is genuinely free.

In Marx's view, the wage bargain, the voluntary exchange of labour power for a wage, resembles this paradigmatically free exchange only superficially. Free wage labour, for Marx, is 'wage slavery', a consequence of capitalist exploitation. What warrants this assessment are the background, institutional circumstances that condition the wage bargain in regimes of private property; circumstances that substantially reproduce the freedom-restricting effects of overt coercion.[24] The worker is formally free not to work, but substantively 'unfree' insofar as the alternative is, in effect, a sanction (though not, as in overtly coercive settings, a sanction deliberately imposed). Were people generally able to realize their wants without labour, then the decision to work, whether for oneself or for others, would resemble the transactions of self-sufficient farmers in the early and rude state of society. Of course, this happy condition cannot be fully attained so long as wants surpass the means for their satisfaction, but it can be approximated.

In the Marxian theory of history, capitalism's mission is to 'revolutionize' production through massive investments in new technologies and other productive resources. But capitalism, in Marx's view, cannot augment the level of development of productive forces indefinitely. Like preceding economic structures, capitalism generates its own debilitating contradictions. As it matures, capitalist production relations increasingly 'fetter' development. Then socialism, which capitalist development makes possible, finally becomes necessary — to liberate the productive forces capitalism vastly augments but cannot indefinitely expand.

To explain why capitalist production relations eventually fetter the development of productive forces, classical Marxism identified processes internal to 'the laws of motion' of the capitalist mode of production. Of these processes, the most important, the tendency for the rate of profit to fall, renders the system increasingly unable to absorb investments. With a rising 'organic composition of capital' — the proportion of 'constant' to 'variable' capital[25] — the rate of profit declines. There are, therefore, ever-diminishing returns on new investments and ever-diminishing incentives to invest. Development is fettered and, in the ensuing crisis, the system itself grinds towards generalized collapse.

Needless to say, this scenario accords poorly with the historical evidence. In addition, its rationale depends on the cogency of Marxian value theory, an analytical system now understood to be radically flawed.[26] Thus Cohen, though reconstructing a version of orthodox historical materialism, expressly avoids appealing to the inevitability of capitalist breakdown, insisting instead that what capitalist social relations come to fetter is not quite the development of productive resources, but their rational deployment — for the satisfaction of the fundamental human interest in emancipation from burdensome toil.[27] Irrational development is still development. Capitalist development may impede or even oppose a fundamental, transhistorical human interest, as Cohen maintains, and still create the material conditions for moving from the realm of necessity into the realm of freedom. Given enough time, even a manifestly deformed route to abundance could succeed in transporting humanity to its desired destination.

If there are no insurmountable obstacles impeding the expansion of productive capacities under capitalism, then so far as the development of productive forces is what matters for communism, there is in principle a capitalist road to communism. Unless capitalist social relations are somehow bound to fetter development in ways that preclude overcoming scarcity to the point where productive activity can be genuinely free, private ownership of society's principal, alienable means of production would not be an obstacle in communism's way. And if capitalism is better able than socialism to develop productive forces effectively, the capitalist road to communism might even be the preferred road — or the only road! These suggestions are at odds, of course, with traditional Marxian expectations. But they could be advanced even by those who would concede, following Cohen, that capitalist develpment can only follow a profoundly irrational course.[28]

Ought communists to be socialists? In part, the answer depends on a comparative assessment of the merits of socialism and capitalism. If socialism is intrinsically superior to capitalism in view of values communists (and others) hold, that would be reason enough for communists to be for socialism and against capitalism — provided socialism is at least as likely as capitalism to lead to communism. If socialism does not fare better than capitalism in comparative assessments — or if it does not seem as likely to make communism materially possible — a pro-socialist position could not be sustained. I have elsewhere compared socialism and capitalism with respect to a number of widely shared values, arguing that, in general, socialism indeed fares better.[29] Without a more precise specification of how socialism and capitalism might be realized in particular institutional arrangements, however, few firm conclusions can be drawn. In any case, socialism's weakest suit relative to its historical rival appears to be with what matters most for rendering communism materially possible: the efficient allocation of resources.[30] These considerations are speculative and largely indeterminate, however. The crux of the case against a capitalist road to communism lies elsewhere.

There are reasons why those who share Marx's vision of communism might be attracted to the prospect of achieving communism without socialism. Disappointment with existing socialism and with the policies of Socialist and Communist parties in capitalist countries is widespread and too often justified. More pertinent to Marxian theory is the realization that capitalism has far from exhausted its creative potentialities and attractions. Indeed, it seems indisputable that, for the foreseeable future, private enterprise will remain necessary for satisfying existing wants.[31] A complete elimination of capitalist relations would therefore detract from overall welfare and necessitate a coercive apparatus for repressing capitalist initiatives to the plain detriment of socialist polities and their prospects for moving in a communist direction. It may also be that a categorical prohibition against individuals capitalizing their assets — in Robert Nozick's expression, a proscription of 'capitalist acts between consenting adults' — would be an indefensible restriction of freedom.[32] Then even those who would grant that capitalism works to the detriment of freedom overall, might nevertheless think the outright proscription of capitalist relations even worse.[33]

I will argue that a good deal more than what historical materialism identifies is requisite for communism. Even if a very high level of development were all that mattered, though, it still would not be enough just that productive forces be massively developed. Social wealth would also have to be distributed in ways that liberate workers and other exploited strata from remediable, institutional constraints on their choices as producers. Excluding capitalist breakdown, there is no reason in principle why even this condition cannot be realized in a capitalist economy. Admittedly, it is unlikely that the required abundance would 'trickle down' sufficiently through the operations of capitalist markets. Workers and other non-capitalists would have to improve their position by collective bargaining and other economic strategies, and an expressly political strategy would also be called for. Social insurance programmes and related welfare state measures would be necessary. Insofar as income levels could be maintained in periods of unemployment, the coercive aspect of the wage bargain would be diminished and autonomy enhanced. However it would be foolhardy to place much hope in traditional welfare state measures, and it is difficult even to imagine welfare state provisions of non-pecuniary benefits of work — like self-actualization and self-esteem. In any case, the welfare state has never been intended to eliminate institutional constraints on workers' choices and would have to change radically even to begin to address this problem.

In principle, though, bolder political measures are conceivable. Outright grants could be distributed directly to individuals. If these grants were sufficiently generous, the satisfaction of basic needs would no longer figure as a background constraint on the choices of economic agents. Then the material condition historical materialism identifies for communism would finally be satisfied. If an individual already adequately provided with the means of life should choose to work for pay, the choice would be genuinely free: motivated perhaps by a desire to consume more than would otherwise be possible or for the reason Marx adduced in the *Economic and Philosophic Manuscripts* – to pursue self-realization through unalienated labour. Labour would have to be radically restructured, of course, and also remunerated substantially, detracting severely from capitalists' profits. If work became sufficiently attractive and remunerative, workers would cease to comprise an underclass and capitalists would cease to exercise economic power over them. At the limit, an individual would become a worker or a capitalist strictly for the intrinsic benefits of each activity. Profits and wages would equilibrate. Capitalist exploitation would therefore end, even if the buying and selling of labour power did not. Insofar as this kind of capitalism is conceivable, it *is* possible for capitalist societies to distribute resources in accord with the historical materialist requirement for communism.

However, this result does not impugn Marxism's pro-socialist, anti-capitalist posture. For so far we have taken only what is politically imaginable into account, not what is feasible. It is plain that there would be political resistance to implementing measures of the sort just suggested and that, for systemic reasons, this resistance would be insurmountable in any likely capitalist polity.

What distinguishes socialism from capitalism is private ownership of society's principal alienable means of production or, in other words, control over society's productive assets. In a capitalist economy, therefore, capitalists can disinvest; capital can flee. Unless capital flight is somehow made even less attractive than political measures designed to neutralize capitalists' power and profits, it is evident that in the face of measures promoting communism, capitalists *will* disinvest and that these measures will therefore be in vain. It is theoretically possible, of course, that conditions favouring disinvestment might not pertain. The whole world might adopt the same measures in concert, rendering capital flight impossible for want of a place to flee. Or development might proceed at such an uneven pace that investment outside the area where a capitalist road to communism is attempted would be even less profitable than within, whatever measures the state tries to implement. It is even conceivable that capitalists might not disinvest for patriotic reasons or for the love of communism. Barring these or other unlikely possibilities though, political measures capable of inaugurating a realm of freedom without first ending capitalism would not be feasible, no matter how well capitalism might fare in furthering material development.

In short, even if we discount economic obstacles blocking a capitalist road to communism, a political obstacle remains: the effective power capitalists enjoy in consequence of what makes them capitalists. This obstacle is, for all practical purposes, ineluctable. Even if a political movement dedicated to neutralizing the institutional power of capital should somehow come to power with overwhelming popular support, it still would not be possible to leap beyond the realm of necessity without undoing capitalism first. So long as capitalism remains in force, a political obstacle in the way of communism remains, no matter what the constellation of forces that controls the state.

The position I have sketched is more in accord with orthodox Marxian views than may at first appear. Historical materialism invests capitalism, not socialism, with the mission of developing productive forces to the point of abundance. Thus even believers in the eventual breakdown of capitalist economies, if they are also historical materialists, should not expect capitalism eventually to impede development so much as to hinder the deployment of productive forces already in place. By the time capitalism comes to 'fetter' development, it will have already massively developed productive forces to the point where the leap into the realm of freedom is materially possible. Socialism's first mission therefore, even in strictest Marxian orthodoxy, is political: to eliminate the power of capital, the last great historical obstacle in the way of genuine freedom.

We need not conclude, however, that communism is impossible so long as there is any private ownership of productive capacities. Properly circumscribed and in the right circumstances, 'capitalist relations between consenting adults' may indeed advance welfare and freedom — and even the prospects for communism. The danger, of course, is that capitalism at the margins of a socialist economy will insinuate itself back into the core, eventually undermining socialism itself. *Pace* Marx, it seems that capitalism has far from exhausted its creative potentialities — even today in those places where it is most 'advanced'. There is no extant body of theory adequate for addressing the questions (including ethical questions) raised by the apparently unavoidable 'prematurity' of socialism, and the treatment of what is evidently a continuing interest in capitalist social relations after capitalism's defeat is perhaps the principal theoretical and practical problem confronting socialists. What follows here will touch on these issues only indirectly.

After this long excursus into historical materialism and its implications for socialism and communism, the elements are now nearly all in place to resume the main line of argument in defence of the end of the state. It will be helpful, therefore, to recall where we were before specifically Marxian themes were introduced, and where we are now.

Rousseau, I argued, supplied a vision of the human community organized as a republic of ends, and Robespierre and his fellow revolutionaries demonstrated the need for a revolutionary state to implement this vision but also, implicitly and unwittingly, the historical impossibility of doing so while class divisions, in the form they confronted them, persist. Then using Tocqueville's and Burke's assessments of the French Revolution as points of departure, some Rousseauean insights into the nature of politics were elaborated, with particular attention to revolutionary politics and to what must be the case for the outcomes of revolutionary endeavours to approximate the objectives that motivate them. This shift of focus brought the question of utopianism to the fore. However none of the authors treated in Part 1 provide any satisfactory insight into what actually is utopian. What was lacking at the end of Part 1 was an historical agenda; a defensible account of historical possibility.

This is precisely what historical materialism provides. After Marx, we can see that the republic of ends *is* realizable provided certain socio-economic conditions are met. In a word, what is needed is socialism, with all socialism presupposes and implies.

But socialism is only a necessary condition for communism and the end of the state. It remains to reflect on sufficient conditions. Again, Rousseau and Marx provide useful points of departure.

7
The Socialist State

Rousseau's state must confront and overwhelm the tendency of individuals to act in accordance with private interests.[1] In no arena is this temptation more threatening than in the popular assemblies where, Rousseau insists, enactments are legitimate if and only if each citizen asks not 'What is best for me?' but 'What is best for the political community of which I am an integral part?' The institutional arrangements and practical political measures Rousseau proposed were motivated, in large part, by his determination to increase the likelihood that voters would interrogate themselves properly. In a word, Rousseau's politics is transformative. The measures he proposed — whether social, political or economic — were concocted with a view to changing human beings in order to make actual what the *de jure* state supposes: the exercise of the general will.

The general will is expressed in the assemblies of the people, but Rousseau did not, in fact, assign a prominent role to collective choice itself in transforming the citizenry. The idea that democratic participation is a 'school' for citizenship is Rousseauean in spirit; but it is not a view Rousseau actually held. Rousseau invested more faith in the transformative power of laws, civil religion and the host of social and political measures he recommended for particular conjunctures. He even seems to have envisaged popular assemblies as brief and occasional affairs, convened to ratify a consensus that always exists notionally and that, in a well-constructed polity, should also exist actually long before votes are taken. Despite his predilection for transformative politics and his commitment to democratic procedures, Rousseau regarded popular assemblies less as schools for forming the general will, than as public spectacles for declaring it.

Perhaps Rousseau was afraid that too much time would be spent in meetings; or that political skills useful for furthering private interests, not civic virtue, would be learned in the popular assemblies. Admittedly, these are serious concerns. Nevertheless it is consistent with the spirit, if not the letter, of Rousseau's politics to impute a transformative role to the popular assemblies. In isolation from a comprehensive programme promoting the generality of the will, democratic participation might indeed debilitate and even detract from virtue. But in conjunction with the rest of the political measures Rousseau proposed — or analogues appropriate for different circumstances — it is a useful supplement. Indeed, the proto-Kantian and non-Kantian strains of Rousseau's political philosophy converge implicitly in the idea of direct, democratic rule: as the mechanism through which the sovereign's will becomes known, and also as a means for making actual what is otherwise only notionally possible. Rousseau did not quite draw this conclusion, but he plainly intimated it in praising the direct popular assemblies of his native Geneva and then upholding Geneva, along with ancient Rome, as a model for the *de jure* state.[2]

The guiding idea is that empowerment through decision-making, particularly when choices have palpable consequences, causes persons to rise to the level of their office. Effective power concentrates attention and focuses the will. In popular assemblies where private wills prevail, political skills conducive to furthering private interests will therefore probably be learned. But where the regime of private interest is already vulnerable in consequence of a host of political measures aimed at suppressing it, voting can have very different effects. It will reinforce the conditions for its own possibility. Genuinely democratic decision-making, based on equal respect for persons as indivisible members of the whole community and directed towards the interests of that community, can be expected to foster the moral and intellectual capacities required for democratic citizenship.

It could be otherwise. It might be, for instance, that democratic forms invariably encourage the formation of elites, and that the exercise of elite power reinforces private wills at the expense of the general will. Or it might be, as liberals would have it, that participation is a burden that detracts from activities more in accord with human nature and more conducive to self-realization. These are empirical claims that cannot be adjudicated here. In a philosophical brief of this sort, I can only allude again to the classical identification of essential humanity with political participation and the plausibility of the case for the beneficial effects of democratic empowerment. As noted already, the case for communism, insofar as it depends upon the positive, transformative consequences of democratic participation, must, to some substantial degree, rest on faith. However, this faith has deep roots in our political culture and its theory; even if it is typically more honoured in the word than in the practise.

In any case, the sovereignty of the general will is, at best, a fiction for those who see pre-communist societies riven by class divisions. It is an idea that masks the reality actual politics must confront. To be sure, the *de jure* state supposes a classless society. But it is a classless society conceived without benefit of a theory that acknowledges classes and their struggles. The state of *The Social Contract* superintends a civil society of small independent producers, each owning their own means of production and each exchanging what is not directly consumed through free, market transactions. It is not socialist, therefore, but (according to the definition I advanced in chapter 6) capitalist, though pre-industrial and without a proletariat. In the historical materialist scheme, this form of capitalism can be conceived but without modern industry and a proletariat, capitalism cannot be realized historically.[3] In a word, Rousseau's proposed order is a utopia, an impossibility in the face of history. Rousseau's advocacy of classlessness is in point, then, but his concept of it is inadequate. His view of the state as a community grounded in the rational will of each individual is prescient but impossible so long as class struggle shapes the course of human history. As Marx insisted, for the entire era extending from pre-capitalist class societies through socialism (the initial stage of communism), the state serves to reproduce class domination and can therefore only be grounded in force. It is only with communism that, as Rousseau envisaged, the state or whatever supercedes it can finally be based on rational cooperation.

Marxian theory effectively explodes the fundamental equivocation of Rousseauean political philosophy, locating his distinct concepts of the state at different points in real historical time. But nothing in Marxian theory impugns Rousseau's intimations of faith in democracy's transformative potentialities. Indeed, I will argue that, like Rousseau, Marx needs to accord considerable confidence in the transformative powers of political institutions generally and that, even more plainly than Rousseau, he ought to value democratic participation. In fact, a strain of Marxian theory, evident especially in some of Marx's writings on politics after the Paris Commune and in Lenin's pre-Revolutionary reflections on the state, is democratic and participationist.[4] It is this (Rousseauean) strain within Marxism that I want to extricate and build upon.

I will maintain that any politics suitable for advancing towards communism must be democratic and must encourage the widest possible mass participation in and control over the institutions that direct society. Rousseau himself promoted democracy primarily as a formal device for insuring the autonomous determination of laws.[5] Marx and Lenin promoted direct democracy primarily as a means for insuring the political dominance of the working class. I would insist, however, that democracy's power to educate and transform be brought to the fore — in theory and practice — for these objectives to have any hope of realization. So, far from opposing democracy, Marxian communism, like Rousseauean sovereignty, requires human beings formed through participation in direct and extensive democratic institutions situated at all the interstices of social life.

Statelessness

The state may be defined according to what it does or according to how it operates. Weber's account of the state as institutionalized (legitimate) violence,[6] is a definition of the second type. This definition is implicitly endorsed by Marx and also, equivocally, by Rousseau.[7] Both Rousseau and Marx also defined the state according to what it does. For Rousseau, the state makes it possible for individuals to become the moral beings they essentially are. It is the condition for the possibility of autonomy and therefore for moral agency and self-realization. What the state does, in Marx's view, is less exalted though integral to his theory of history: it organizes the economically dominant class as a ruling class – overcoming internal divisions that would otherwise decapacitate it for domination and encouraging decapacitating internal divisions within subordinate classes.

The state achieves this end through its various institutions, through an historically specific apparatus. It is a tenet of Marxian political theory that the nature of this apparatus will vary according to the kind of political economic system the state superintends. Thus there is a distinctively capitalist state and also, Marx thought, a distinctive form of the state appropriate for socialism.[8] Unfortunately, Marx joined these positions with the orthodox historical materialist claim for the inevitability of communism. His account of the apparatus of different state forms is therefore, to some degree, a misleading fusion of independent positions. In consequence, Marxists have been wont to identify the socialist state in transition to communism with the socialist state as such; confounding proposals for the apparatus of the former with an account of the general form of the latter.

Classical Marxism regards what follows capitalism as the first stage of an historical epoch that ends with communism, a society without a state. However we know that statelessnes admits of several distinct understandings. Insofar as the state is conceived according to its functions, the end of the state just means the end of the institutions that perform those functions, understood in some appropriately general and encompassing sense. Insofar as the state is defined by its essentially violent means, the end of the state suggests the advent of a social order in which individuals' behaviour is coordinated freely and co-operatively, without external force. Then communist statelessness would mean the absence of public, coercive force; the definitive withering away of the state.

Rousseau held that the *de jure* state actually could be realized, taking 'men as they are', but not perfectly. There is no reason to think differently of communism. Marx's ideal community, like Rousseau's, may find it expedient, from time to time, to use violence against its recalcitrant members, in order better to implement genuinely common objectives. The 'moral and collective body' founded by the social contract and implemented historically in Marxian communism can suffer from a collective weakness of will in consequence of human resistance to full rational self-determination. Public force, in this case, can be deployed as an antidote. But the antidote is not the basis of the political community. In short, communist societies, like the *de jure* state, may use force, but they are not grounded in force. In contrast to class societies, force is not a means for forging a collective will.

If the state is defined by what Marx deemed its principal function — the political organization of class domination — it follows trivially that under communism, a classless society, there would be no state. Insofar as communism is possible or (as the orthodox maintain) inevitable, then so too is the end of the state in this sense. If the state apparatus is understood to encompass only those institutional forms that are proper for states in class societies, then it would also be likely, if not strictly necessary, that under communism this apparatus would wither away for want of a sufficient reason. By envisaging the *de jure* state in a society without classes, Rousseau would have exactly anticipated the end of the state in the first, more general, sense. However, lacking a theory of classes and therefore of institutional arrangements in class societies, Rousseau could have no notion of the end of the state in the second, more particular, sense.

More interesting and contentious is the idea of the end of the state as a coercive apparatus. Rousseau suggested this idea without quite endorsing it,[9] and it is plain that Marxists intend it in predicting the withering away of the state. On the face of it, the prospect seems hopelessly utopian. But it can fairly be construed in a way that is not nearly so unlikely. The end of the state as a coercive apparatus need not imply the complete termination of public coercion as such. Communist societies need not be perfectly cooperative associations, but only communities based on rational cooperation. A community of rational cooperators could decide, as it were, to use force against itself. What is predicted, then, is not quite the end of public coercion, but a radical transformation (and corresponding diminution) of its role. Rousseau, in the end, finally withdrew from predicting an end of the state: Marx was not so hesitant. By becoming clearer than either writer was about what the end of the state involves, we can see that these positions are not, after all, so far apart.

The Pre-communist State

Marx's name for the state that leads the transition to communism and therefore to the end of the state itself was 'the dictatorship of the proletariat'. The name is apt, but unfortunate and likely to mislead. In order not to be misled, it will be helpful to reflect on Marx's insistence, against the anarchists, that states – communities grounded in force – continue to be necessary in the period between the overthrow of capital and the full emergence of communism. After a victorious socialist revolution, there will be deeply entrenched but historically superseded institutions that may require generations to overcome. Religion and perhaps also the family are examples. But, in Marx's view, the pre-communist state is not just a vestige of earlier social orders, requiring time to cast off. Within socialism, the state has a mission to perform; a mission for which there is no parallel under capitalism or in any preceding historical epoch. The pre-communist state is indispensable for superintending the transition to communism and, in so doing, creating the conditions for its own demise.

After a socialist revolution, perhaps for an indefinite period, it will be necessary to have an organized force for defending socialism against counter-revolution – waged from outside the borders of the new, socialist society or from within, by the former deposed ruling class and its allies. But, in Marx's view, a state would be necessary under socialism, regardess of security interests. It would be necessary even if socialism were somehow to triumph simultaneously on a world scale and without significant opposition. A state is required to organize and superintend the dissolution of everything, including forms of exploitation, that detract from autonomy. More generally, a state is indispensable for administering a social order in transition to a classless society. But perhaps its most important function is to make people capable of pursuing and maintaining communist ways. Like individuals emerging from a state of nature, the citizens of a recently established socialist society, formed under capitalism and encumbered with the legacy of their formation, cannot yet be members of a republic of ends. The final historical mission of the state is to reverse this psychological obstacle in the way of a communist future by forging communist men and women in the crucible of its institutions. To this end, radical and direct democracy is, I submit, its most potent weapon.

The socialist state is necessary, then, for defence, for administration and for education. To seek to abolish the state immediately is to deny these necessities. But these necessities are liable to transformation through the operations of the state itself to the point that the state, as an institution grounded in force, can finally be rendered unnecessary. Anarchism, then, is not mistaken in its objectives, but only premature in its attempt to implement them. Anarchists are at fault, if at all, only in their impatience, an impatience sound political theory can correct and wise practice can overcome. To this end, all the institutions of society, including the popular assemblies, must combine together. Then as transformative politics works its effects, as people are progressively changed, what makes states necessary will be progressively undone. Following Rousseau's lead and Marx's and Lenin's indications, it is fair to insist on the paramount role of democratic participation in this monumental process of transformation. By democratizing itself, the pre-communist state alters the conditions of its existence ('taking men as they are') and organizes its own *Aufhebung*.

The Dictatorship of the Proletariat

To hold, as Marx sometimes did, that states are always dictatorships is plainly false if dictatorship is understood to designate a form of government in which an individual or group of individuals rules at is own discretion without impediment from parliamentary or judicial institutions. But this customary understanding is not quite what Marx intended.[10] Thus Marx, and Lenin after him, declared representative democracy, ostensibly dictatorship's antonym, the characteristic form of the class dictatorship of the bourgeoisie, and they took the Paris Commune, hardly a dictatorship in the received sense, as the nearest historical approximation of the dictatorship of the proletariat. In Rousseauean terms, the dictatorship of the proletariat pertains to the state, not the government. The claim, then, is that state power — always, in the Marxian view, the power of a social class or coalition of classes — rests ultimately on force; not law, not custom, and certainly not the rational will of the governed. The terminology is misleading and deviant, but the thought is familiar. The idea that force is the foundation of states is, again, the dominant view in western political theory from Macchiavelli through Hobbes to Weber and beyond. What is distinctively Marxian is the additional claim that the state is always the dictatorship of a class.

Hobbes's account of the foundation of the state is exemplary and also pertinent to the argument that follows. In Hobbes's view, individuals in a state of nature are incapable of achieving stable patterns of cooperation in accord with their interests. By pursuing their interests, they produce radically sub-optimal outcomes, relative to the interests that motivate them. The state of nature is therefore 'a war of all against all', in which individuals' ends are seldom, if ever, realized and life itself is 'solitary, poor, nasty, brutish and short'.[11] Order is possible only with states, that is, with an apparatus for coordinating behaviour coercively. In more contemporary terms: the problem the state solves is a generalized Prisoners' Dilemma, where the pay-off structure individuals confront is such that, if individuals act rationally by maximizing utility, their pay-offs are worse than they might otherwise be. The state solves the problem by constraining maximizing behaviour through sanctions or, in other words, by changing the pay-off structure.

Marxian political theory implicitly takes over this characterization of the state's task, but in a way that accords with the substantive claims of historical materialism. For Hobbes, society is a collection of atomic individuals. For Marx, the fundamental societal units for purposes of political theory are social classes. Atomic individuals in a Hobbesian state of nature bear generally antagonistic relations with one another, but are relatively equal in power.[12] Likewise, classes generally oppose one another. But there is no parallel, in Marx's account, to the relative equality of the antagonistic parties. There are, instead, the exploited and their exploiters. However something like Hobbes's coordination problem remains: not primarily for individuals as such, but for individuals within social classes. Marx's solution recalls Hobbes's. The state is the means by which the dominant class overcomes its coordination problem, its 'war of all against all', the better to wage 'war', i.e. class war, against those it dominates. It is the means by which the exploiting class organizes its class dictatorship.

Coordination problems confronted by subordinate classes are therefore exacerbated by the dominant class's solution to its coordination problem. In Marx's view and even more explicitly in Lenin's, the revolutionary party is useful for countering the state's role in decapacitating subordinate classes, just as it is indispensable in the struggle for state power. But it is only with the conquest of state power that the coordination problems of subordinate classes can be definitively redressed. It is by organizing its own class dictatorship that a previously subordinate class fully becomes a 'class for itself'.[13]

Joined with the orthodox historical materialist claim for the inevitability of communism, these positions explain Marx's and Lenin's identification of the state under socialism with the dictatorship of the proletariat. This tenet of Marxian orthodoxy is embarrassing for Marxists claiming allegiance to democracy. But embarrassment on this count, thought understandable, is unjustified. The orthodox position is contentious, but it is not anti-democratic. It is worth reflecting on what actually is contentious in the orthodox view. The description of the state as a dictatorship, though contestable, is virtually commonplace. The view that states are always class dictatorships is more contentious, but no more so than the historical materialist theses upon which it is based. What is very contentious, even from a Marxian vantage-point, is the additional claim, the distinctive contribution of historical materialist orthodoxy, that the class whose dictatorship is exercised under socialism is always and can only be the proletariat.

Again, the dictatorship of the proletariat is not a form of government, but a type of state: a state superintending the transition to communism or, what comes to the same thing in the Marxian scheme, a state where the working class holds state power.[14] Plainly, workers' power does not imply à dictatorial form of government. However it does imply restrictions on the rights of former exploiters and other social strata whose interests are detrimental to workers' interests. If it is true that states are always class dictatorships, then genuinely equal citizenship is impossible, in any case, so long as states exist. Representative democracies, class dictatorships of the bourgeoisie, proclaim equality the better to organize the domination of the many by the few. Proletarian class dictatorships, more transparently, proclaim inequality — to the advantage of the many and the detriment of the few — in order to superintend the transition to a classless society where equality for all is finally achieved.

It should hardly be necessary to add that workers' power does not imply the institutional forms that emerged during the revolutionary upheavals in which capitalism was overthrown and still less the institutions of existing socialism. No socialist polity has ever been a model, though some may once have been examples. The most likely candidate is, of course, post-Revolutionary Russia. But the most that can be said, even for the Russian case, is that, in the extraordinary and unfortunate circumstances confronted by the first successful proletarian revolution, a particular form of proletarian class dictatorship was established. There would be no immediate implications for institutions in post-capitalist states born in different, more propitious circumstances.

The proletariat may be the principal agent of socialist revolution, as Marx and Lenin believed. But *pace* Marx and Lenin, it need not be the ruling class under socialism. Quite the contrary. In view of the persistence of exploitation under socialism, there is good reason — in Marxian political theory — to expect the socialist state to be a class dictatorship of the principal exploiters under socialism. If historical experience is a guide, it is likely to be a dictatorship of the incumbents of high state, party and bureaucratic positions.

The proletariat can come to hold state power in consequence of a political victory over its former exploiters. But then the proletariat must struggle to retain state power against the tendency of post-capitalist social relations to engender a new ruling class. It must dominate its exploiters politically; using the state to work against the interests of the beneficiaries of the property relations the state superintends. Thus the dictatorship of the proletariat, though hardly the outrageous idea commonly supposed, is a plain anomaly in Marxian theory. So far from being a political superstructure in accord with its economic base, it opposes its base; not in consequence of an emerging 'contradiction' between forces and relations of production, but in its very principle. However nothing less anomalous is capable of ending in communism. It is tempting therefore to conclude that the idea itself is untenable, if not incoherent: contradicting fundamental tenets of Marxian political theory and also reasonable, common-sense expectations.[15] However it is wise to resist the temptation.

Marxian descriptions of the dictatorship of the proletariat consist largely of speculations on its apparatus. This focus is well chosen, though it can be misleading. Proletarian class rule does not strictly require a particular form of state apparatus. But there are important ramifications for state institutions when the proletariat controls the state. Since the proletariat has no interest in maintaining its position as a proletariat, state institutions in a proletarian class dictatorship will be contrived in order not to reproduce themselves indefinitely, but instead to undo progressively the conditions for their possibility. In a general way, this exigency has implications for institutional arrangements.

For Marx as for Rousseau, there are no universally applicable directives or technical manipulations sufficient for bringing about the objectives of their respective politics. There are only measures, appropriate or not in different conjunctures. Marx's reflections on politics, like Rousseau's, were attuned to the specificity of these conjunctures. But to this end, historical materialism is of little help. It specifies only material constraints on political undertakings. What is needed, however, is a fine-tuned appreciation of prevailing circumstances and a sensitivity to the extra-material constraints Tocqueville and Burke faulted the French Revolutionaries for ignoring. In Marx, as in Rousseau, political theory and reflections on politics are, if not quite opposed, at least in some considerable tension. It could hardly be otherwise insofar as political theory demands a level of abstraction remote from ordinary political concerns. For Rousseau, the social contract is everywhere and always the same but the execution of its terms requires sensitivity to circumstance and the artful adaptation of principle to practice. Marxian politics demands no less.

Still, theory can provide general indications. We owe perhaps the most helpful indications to Lenin.[16] Despite his obvious departures from Rousseau's express proposals, Lenin effectively generalized the democratic intuition that motivated Rousseau's politics. However Lenin's reflections are not so much theoretical as practical. Like Rousseau in his non-Kantian moments, Lenin theorized by proposing specific measures for particular conjunctures. The measures he proposed fall into two principal categories. First are those that aim at the suppression of parliamentarism in all its forms and its replacement by an administrative system of workers', soldiers', and peasants' councils (soviets). Then there are measures that aim at the destruction of the representative apparatus characteristic of bourgeois states: standing armies, paramilitary police, independent judiciaries, and their replacement by institutions of direct popular rule: militias, an armed citizenry, peoples' tribunals. The idea in each case is to augment popular power by extending popular control in all the spheres of social, political and economic life. Thus democracy is both instrumental for forming communists and indispensable administratively. Only radical, direct democracy can counter the tendency for new ruling classes to form and consolidate their domination. As the socialist order is democratized, the power attendant upon continuing inequalities in the distribution of productive assets is neutralized. So, far from reproducing remaining exploitative relations indefinitely, a democratized state can therefore be used to undo the conditions that make remaining forms of exploitation a threat to a communist future. Radical, popular democracy, including the proletariat and its allies in the direction of the state, is the general means for preventing the reassertion of social relations inimical to the construction of communism and also, above all, for transforming the proletariat and its allies into the human material necessary for that task. In short, the dictatorship of the proletariat — where the working class holds state power and wields it to build a communist future — is radical democracy for the overwhelming majority, the working class and its allies under socialist conditions.

Typically, epochal historical change is inaugurated under political regimes controlled by representatives of insurgent classes. Correspondence between base and superstructure is established later when, through the exercise of state power, new social relations of production are definitively established. The dictatorship of the proletariat is a revolutionary order in just this sense, but in a revolution for communism. If it appears anomalous, it is in virtue of its location in the historical trajectory. In relation to states born in bourgeois revolutions, the dictatorship of the proletariat differs qualitatively in duration and outcome. The great bourgeois revolutions were events of relatively brief duration in which a new social order, already born and partially matured, acquired a proper state. History has shown that capitalism too can be overthrown by revolutionary events; subordinate classes or their representatives (real or imagined) can capture the state and use it to eliminate capitalist exploitation. However, a genuinely communist revolution cannot be waged this way. Communism does not mature in the womb of the old society, but must be forged *ab initio* after the old order has been broken — through deliberate, political direction. In this crucial respect, communism differs radically from other forms of socialism. If it is realizable at all, it can only be in consequence of an historically protracted struggle, a process of indefinite duration. Socialism is necessary in this endeavour but not sufficient.[17] What is required beyond socialism is the dictatorship of the proletariat. A politics that aims at communism is therefore always a revolutionary and democratic politics — a struggle in and over the state and throughout the social order for democracy. In this vast historical undertaking, the overthrow of capitalism and the establishment of workers' power are only fragile, first steps.

This is not to say that an indefinitely prolonged combination of 'virtue and terror' is the price humanity must pay for communism.[18] Except perhaps at the moment of rupture with capitalism, when conditions most resemble familiar revolutionary events, Jacobin — or Bolshevik — practice is not exemplary. The point, after all, is to educate, not to repress. It is the radical democracy of the *de jure* state, not the administrative processes of the Great and Red Terrors, that is calculated to maintain workers' power and to form the human material communism requires. Robespierre was indeed a trenchant, if unwitting, critic of Rousseau. He perceived, as Rousseau did not, the inexorable reality of class struggle.[19] But once Robespierre's lesson had been learned and elaborated by Marx and his followers, Rousseau has the last word.

The feasibility of a communist revolution depends therefore on the extent to which the state can operate independently of the economic base it superintends. In this regard, historical materialism is not encouraging, even if it is not definitively opposed. Again, it is Rousseauean political philosophy — and the strain of Marxism that joins Rousseauean themes — that supports more optimistic prognostications. Needless to say, it is of the utmost importance for any genuinely communist politics that optimistic prognostications be supportable.

State Autonomy

For the dictatorship of the proletariat and therefore communism to be possible, proletarian class rule must not only be materially possible but also institutionally feasible; the proletariat must be able to constitute itself as a ruling class and reproduce its domination for as long as the construction of communism requires. Only then would communism be on the historical agenda in the sense that means for its realization can be conceived 'taking men as they are and laws as they might be'.

In the historical materialist scheme, so long as social relations of production are stably reproduced, the economic base in some (strong but nevertheless vague) sense determines legal and political superstructures. Then the dominant economic class is also the politically dominant class, the ruling class. This claim holds for all historical periods that are not transitional. It therefore holds for pre-capitalist class societies, for capitalism and also for most socialisms. But the normal relation of base and superstructure will not hold for that form of socialism that is the first phase of communism. Pre-communist socialism is permanently in transition, permanently revolutionary.

At the level of abstraction at which it is pitched, historical materialism is strictly agnostic with respect to how the economically dominant class rules. Arguably, though, the theory does suggest 'instrumentalist' views that deny the state any significant independence from the economically dominant class. Instrumentalism is supported by a number of celebrated Marxian formulations, of which the best known is the claim in *The Communist Manifesto* that 'the executive of the modern State is but a committee for managing the common affairs of the whole bourgeoisie'. Marx himself, particularly in the decade of the 1840s, advanced instrumentalist views.[20] He also advanced non-instrumentalist positions after 1850 and, again, in the 1870s in his reflections on the Paris Commune.[21] But whatever Marx may have said at one time or another, instrumentalism is not entailed by his theory of history. If Marx is to be drawn upon for a consistent, communist politics, it is fortunate that it is not. Communism is conceivable only on a non-instrumentalist account of the relation between base and superstructure. To sustain the political orientation that motivates it, Marxism must be capable of ascribing relative autonomy to political processes generally, and to the state in particular.

Marx nowhere directly addresses the question of the independence of political from economic practices, though many of his historical investigations, his reflections on politics and even some of his casual remarks made in passing in other contexts bear on the question. However it would be useless to attempt to tease a full-fledged theory out of all the pertinent textual material. Marxian theory has little to say in general about the autonomy of the state. Typically, Marx's remarks on state autonomy involve finer-grained assessments of historical situations than historical materialism or Marxian political theory provide. His theory — if 'theory' is the right word for an atheoreticism reminiscent of mainstream historical writing — is just that state autonomy is conditioned by ever-varying circumstances. At times, the instrumentalist picture will pertain. At times, it will not. As Marx's historical writings show, the differences are explicable in principle by the ordinary methods of historical analysis, not by the invocation of fundamental tenets of a general theory of history.[22]

Still, the dictatorship of the proletariat cannot fail to raise difficulties for historical materialists. A proletarian class dictatorship uses the power it wields against the beneficiaries of socialist production relations. In this sense, it is absolutely, not relatively, autonomous. Absolute autonomy, however, is problematic. Historical materialism may not imply instrumentalism, but it is difficult to reconcile with anti-instrumentalism. The dictatorship of the proletariat, however, is an anti-instrumentalist state. Evidently, the sense of anomaly the concept evokes is not quite dissipated, even after it is disentangled from unlikely orthodox strictures. To defend the dictatorship of the proletariat within Marxian theory, it is therefore necessary to reflect further on the constraints economic systems impose on states.

Again, Marx's writings are not directly helpful. Marx did show, in discussing capitalist states, that there can be a wide range of variation in actual degrees of state autonomy. He even thought it possible for the bourgeoisie to abdicate political power, as in the France of Louis Bonaparte, when doing so serves its interests. But even in its abdications, the interests of the economically dominant class continue to be served. Capitalists may exercise political power more or less directly or not exercise it at all but, in the long run, the state cannot be used against their interests.

It is natural to describe this limit on state autonomy in functionalist terms: the (capitalist) state is constrained in its degree of independence because it functions to reproduce and reinforce (capitalist) production relations. It is clear, moreover, how this functional relation is achieved. The pertinent consideration has already been adduced in arguing for the necessity of socialism for communism.[23] The capitalist state will generally serve capitalists' interests in consequence of what distinguishes capitalism from socialism: the power private ownership of alienable means of production confers.

Under capitalism, there is real (not merely juridical) private ownership of non-human productive resources. Typically, capitalists do not control these resources directly, but instead delegate management responsibilities. Final authority, however, always rests with the real owners. Capitalists therefore control the deployment of means of production, just as they control the surplus generated in the production process. We know that capitalists face potentially debilitating intra-class coordination problems, but that these problems are in principle soluble, allowing capitalists to act as a class. Sometimes coordination will emerge as an unintended consequence of individual capitalists' choice. But, in general, political intervention will be necessary to ensure that capitalists' class interests are advanced. By whatever combination of means, so long as internal divisions are sufficiently overcome, capitalists are able to ensure that their collective interests are addressed — through the power they exercise in virtue of what they own. In a word, capitalists can always 'strike': they can disinvest or under-utilize means of production. Therefore no capitalist state can work for long against the interests of property owners. An errant state, should it assault capitalists' interests, will find the society it superintends at risk of economic disintegration. In this way, capitalists constrain what states do, even when they do not control the state. The degree of state autonomy will vary, but it will always be limited by the power private ownership of society's principal means of production confers on the economically dominant class.

Socialist property relations also concentrate power in the hands of particular individuals: skills and organizational exploiters. In principle, these individuals, like capitalists, can strike or otherwise under-utilize the resources they control. It would therefore seem that there is a structural constraint on the autonomy of socialist states, analogous to the constraint capitalist states confront. But there is a qualitative difference. Under capitalism, ownership of productive assets confers power distinct from — and analytically prior to — state power. The state superintends the rules of the game. It may even become a player in its own right. But the economic system, in the familiar Marxian metaphor, is still the base upon which the state rises as a superstructure. After capitalism, the economy is policitized, even when it is not democratized. The base/superstructure metaphor therefore becomes problematic. The economic system may still account for the political superstructure, as historical materialism asserts; but economic power no longer underlies political power. Social relations of production therefore become amenable to political transformation to a degree unprecendented in capitalist societies. Under socialism, then, there is no need for an epochal transformation, a social revolution, to overcome skills and organizational exploitation. What is required instead is a sustained political revolution — for democracy. Herein lies the condition for the possibility in Marxian theory for the dictatorship of the proletariat and thereby also for communism itself.

The socialist state should be vastly more capable than any capitalist state of acting against the tendency of prevailing property relations without incurring the withdrawal of productive resources. To be sure, skills exploiters might refuse to deploy or develop the skills they 'own'. But if human nature is at all educable in the way Rousseau and his Marxian followers supposed, if civic virtue can be fostered, it should be eminently possible to wean human beings away from a motivational structure that makes skills exploitation necessary for the deployment of skills. Rousseau, again, inadvertently showed the way. What is required is a concerted political effort on behalf of communal solidarity and for simplicity of *moeurs*, the psychological prerequistes for the exercise of the general will. Democratic participation must, I think, play a prominent role in this endeavour. Popular assemblies, where citizens deliberate disinterestedly and count equally in the determination of social choices, are models for disinterestedness and egalitarianism in all spheres, including the economic. When individuals become genuinely indivisible parts of a 'moral and collective body', they will be indisposed, as citizens, to take advantage of endowments that, by common consensus, are arbitrary from the stand-point of distributive justice. As the sphere of citizenship is extended into all the interstices of social life, this disposition will, in all likelihood, become generalized. Perhaps persons will even be disposed to pool the fruits of the labours they perform in order to promote egalitarian outcomes; in other words, to end skills exploitation even in cases where offences to justice are less pronounced or non-existent.

These expectations depend on social psychological

assumptions that are, admittedly, disputable. But skills exploitation, even if insurmountable, is unlikely to elicit substantial constraints on state autonomy or otherwise affect the politics of socialist states significantly. Control over organizational assets is overwhelmingly more troublesome in existing socialist countries and in any likely socialism. However this form of control over productive resources, unlike the form conferred by private ownership, exists only at the sufferance of (socialist) states. Organizational exploiters, like capitalists, can wield the state apparatus as an 'instrument'. In existing socialist countries, organizational exploiters are, in fact, recruited through the state and party apparatus to such a degree that the distinction between state and party functionaries and non-state hierarchs has become virtually meaningless. But since the power of incumbents of commanding positions, unlike the power of capitalists, is derivative, organizational exploitation is much more amenable than capitalist exploitation to state-directed measures for its democratization. It may be utopian to expect, even in the long run, that organizational hierarchies can be eliminated entirely. But it surely is possible for a proletarian class dictatorship to eliminate — or severely mitigate — differential returns based on incumbency of positions and, more importantly, to circumscribe the power that follows from control of this asset. Even a non-democratic, socialist state can subordinate the interests of its hierarchs to its own, as may have occurred in the Soviet Union under Stalin. Organizational exploitation looks insurmountable in existing socialist countries precisely because these states are not proletarian class dictatorships. They are, more likely, dictatorships of organizational exploiters or, what comes to the same thing, of the political class. If political power were set against organizational exploiters as happens, by hypothesis, when the working class wields state power, the situation would be radically altered. So, far from appearing insurmountable, organizational exploitation would seem eminently vulnerable.

The difference between socialism and capitalism is not, as pro-socialists sometimes claim, that socialism democratizes the economy, while capitalism permits, at most, only the democratization of the state. Socialism can indeed democratize the economy and, if communism is to be its outcome, it must. But socialism can also be non-democratic economically and politically. The real difference is that socialism politicizes the economy by eliminating the power of capital. It therefore restructures the distinction, fundamental to all capitalist societies, between the economic order and its superintending political regime. This is the condition *sine qua non* for the degree of state autonomy required for the dictatorship of the proletariat and therefore for communism.

Concluding Note

Traditionally, Marxists have advanced the view I have also defended: that the transition from socialism to communism is an intra-epochal change, not a transformation from one mode of production to another. But Marxists have also endorsed what I have denied: the appropriateness of the base/superstructure metaphor under socialism holding that, after capitalism, the state continues to depend upon prevailing economic relations, just as it did in preceding historical epochs. These positions can coexist only by denying that the working class under socialism is an economically subordinated, exploited class. For reasons already adduced,[24] it is plain that this view cannot be sustained so long as skills and organizational exploitation continue.

An alternative position could acknowledge the exploitation of the working class under socialism, but also retain the traditional view of the relation between base and superstructure. It would then follow, as noted, that the socialist state cannot be autonomous in the way I have suggested. Rather, like capitalist states, it would be structurally constrained. The threat of disinvestment renders capitalist states only relatively autonomous at best; the threat of under-utilization of organizational assets (and perhaps also skills) would similarly constrain state freedom under socialism. Then communism, if possible at all, would require a revolution against socialism: an inter-epochal transformation or, in more traditional terminology, a social, not merely a political, revolution. This understanding is suggested moreover by the identification of epochal transformations with the elimination of forms of exploitation. If the elimination of capitalist exploitation is tantamount to the epochal transition from capitalism to socialism, then surely the end of the forms of exploitation proper to socialism amount to an epochal transformation as well.

It should be noted that so far as my objective is just to defend the cogency and possibility of communist statelessness, I could well accede to this alternative conceptualization. What does it matter, after all, how the revolutionary change required to move beyond 'the realm of necessity' is called? What matters is how this protracted and far-reaching transformation is conceived; and what there is to say about revolutionary states in transition to communism can presumably be maintained on either view.

Nevertheless, it does matter which formulation is adopted. It matters, obviously, for theories of state autonomy and for accounts of the similarities and differences between capitalist and non-capitalist states. It matters for the identification of socialism with post-capitalism; a characterization that, I have argued, is both defensible and fruitful.[25] And it matters for the analysis of 'existing socialism' and the host of issues that cluster around this problem.[26] These topics, especially the last, are at some remove from the question of the end of the state. But they are among the stakes in the debate I have had to join in order to defend that idea.

This is not the place to pursue debates orthogonal to the principal subject of this book, beyond what is necessary to make a case for the end of the state. But in view of the fact that the stance I have proposed in defence of statelessness differs from both the traditional Marxian view and from a likely criticism of the traditional view, it is appropriate, if only to anticipate debates to come, to conclude this discussion by drawing my position into sharp focus.

What I have argued for accords with the spirit and letter of traditional Marxism in viewing socialism and communism as stages of the same epochal historical structure; and with the spirit but not the letter of traditional Marxism in acknowledging the existence of exploitation under socialism. However it accords with neither the spirit nor the letter of received Marxian views in maintaining that, with the elimination of capitalist social relations, the state is structurally unconstrained by the economic base it superintends. I have argued, however, that near-total state autonomy is a condition for the possibility of moving from socialism to communism and the end of the state. In other words, I have maintained that, after capitalism, there are still exploiters and perhaps even social classes based on exploitation relations, but denied that when exploiters hold state power under socialism (and turn the state away from communism), they do so in consequence of the social relations of production from which they benefit. I have held instead that, after capitalism, economic power, insofar as it is distinguishable from state power, derives from the state itself; from the grip the 'political class' exercises over the state and party apparatus.

The productive asset skills exploiters hold is too widely distributed and too dependent upon societal nurturing to serve as a basis for class formation. The relative equality of persons in the distribution of natural endowments and the interdependence of persons in the development and deployment of innate talents renders skills exploitation benign. Organizational exploitation is another matter. In all likelihood, hierarchically structured organizations cannot be eliminated without diminishing the level of productivity below the threshold where socialism would become materially impossible. But I have argued, even so, that control over organizational assets is a political artifact, and that this control does not constitute an independent base of power. The fact that, in principle, both capitalists and organizational exploiters can withdraw the assets they control is a formal similarity masking a difference of paramount importance for political theory and socialist practice.

It is easy to be misled by existing socialism. I would suggest that existing socialist societies are party dictatorships, organized and maintained by those who have seized state power (in organized insurrections or through military imposition) and continued by new members recruited into party, government and military institutions. It is these institutions that sustain organizational exploitation as a by-product of control of the state. Capitalists' power, on the other hand, is prior to state power and supported by it. For this reason, capitalists stand in a very different relation to the state than do organizational exploiters, with implications for state autonomy that I have tried to trace. After capitalism, state and society are not separated in the old way. Insofar as a distinction can still be conceived, economic power more nearly depends on state power than vice versa.

This description of existing socialism is intended only to illustrate what I have claimed about socialist states: that they need not be proletarian class dictatorships, that they are in fact liable to seizure by organized groups and that, unlike pre-socialist states, they are not constrained by underlying production relations. I have not offered evidence in support of my description of existing socialism, and I concede that my description might be mistaken. Contrary to what I have supposed, organizational exploiters might in fact control productive assets independently of the power the political class holds over the state. But then organizational exploiters would also be capitalist exploiters in a new guise, for they would, in fact if not in law, own the assets they command. Then, to comprehend existing socialism, it would be necessary to expand our understanding of capitalism — to accommodate unprecedented juridical and political forms that seem to accord with an economic structure quite different from the structure actually in place. What would require modification, in short, is not the proposed identification of socialism with post-capitalism, but the received understanding of capitalism itself. To count as post-capitalist, it is not enough for a social order to have broken juridically with traditional capitalist forms. A social order is post-capitalist if and only if it has eliminated capitalist exploitation.

Communists and orthodox Trotskyists have deemed the Soviet Union and other existing socialist countries workers' states, disagreeing only on the extent, if any, of their 'deformations'. Other Trotskyists, Maoists and some independent Marxists have called these countries capitalist or state capitalist. And it has sometimes been claimed that the Soviet Union and the rest are neither capitalist nor socialist, but something else not recognized in standard historical materialist accounts. My position is at odds with each of these views. I have suggested — I think with considerable justification — that the workers' state and state capitalist descriptions are at odds with the facts. But these characterizations are at least consistent with the body of theory I have defended. The claim that existing socialist countries are neither capitalist nor socialist, though motivated by the facts of the matter, is at odds with defensible historical materialist positions. Arguably, historical materialism could be modified yet again to accommodate a variety of post-capitalist economic structures. But I have already said enough to suggest why I think it wise to resist this particular modification.

8
Communism and the State

For Marx, the state is the means through which economically dominant classes overcome their intra-class coordination problems and organize their domination of subordinate classes. It is through the state that society's principal exploiters become a ruling class. The state, then, can only be a class state; and politics, by definition, is a form of class struggle. If the end of class society is materially possible and also institutionally feasible, it follows immediately that the state and politics generally can be transcended. With the end of classes, the state and politics will end too. But Marx also joined mainstream western political theory in construing the state according to its means: as the institutionalization of (*de facto*) legitimate violence. However considerations that support the end of the state in the former sense, after communism is achieved, do not in any obvious way entail the end of the state in this vastly more contentious sense. The end of classes and class struggle would not end the need for institutionalizing a means of violence capable of addressing the overwhelmingly debilitating coordination problems identified perspicuously by Rousseau and Hobbes before him. It therefore seems that Marx's case for the end of the state proves much less than it purports to show; that Marxian theory supports the idea that the state, understood as a means for organizing class domination, can pass away for want of classes to dominate and be dominated, but nothing more.

This conclusion, however, is too sweeping. Despite the manifest confusion that plagues the traditional formulation, the end of the state in the first sense does bear on its withering away in the second. In defence of this claim, Rousseau again provides a point of departure.

For Rousseau, as for Marx, private interest cannot be vanquished so long as classes remain; the end of classes — indeed, the end of all social divisions prone to foster 'private wills' — is necessary for the realization of a republic of ends. But the republic of ends and the *de jure* state converge in Rousseau's thought; ostensibly, the social contract would establish a republic of ends, but for the need to deal with recalcitrants. For Rousseau, then, the end of class divisions and class struggle is necessary not only for the end of the state but also for its beginning: the *de jure* state cannot exist so long as class divisions remain. What classical Marxism considered sufficient for ending the state is, in Rousseau's view, a condition for the possibility of the state itself.

The difference, however, is more apparent than real; and, for thinking about the viability of statelessness as an ideal, it is helpful to undo the deception. What makes the state necessary and possible, according to *The Social Contract*, are trans-historical aspects of the human condition (relative equality in the distribution of mental and physical endowments, geographical proximity, relative scarcity) and historically relative aspects of human nature (culminating in the emergence and predominance of *amour propre*). Given a state of nature so conceived, 'the fundamental problem of political life' becomes 'to find a form of association that defends and protects the person and goods of each associate with all the common force, and by means of which each one, uniting with all, nevertheless obeys only himself and remains as free as before.' The social contract provides the 'solution': each individual and his forces must be 'put in common under the supreme direction of the general will'.[1] It will be instructive to consider how historical materialism alters Rousseau's 'fundamental problem' and its solution.

The 'Fundamental Problem' Historicized

Rousseau faulted Hobbes for misconceiving autonomy and not acknowledging its proper importance as a priceless and essential attribute that legitimate political institutions must always protect and never transgress or even jeopardize. This difference apart, Rousseau thought Hobbes had got the 'fundamental problem' right; that he had correctly described the condition of human beings without a state — in a state of nature — immediately prior to the social contract.

Hobbes's state of nature has an objective and subjective side. Relative equality (resulting in mutual vulnerability), geographical proximity and relative scarcity are objective circumstances; aspects of the human condition, independent of the dispositions human beings evince as subjects. 'Human nature', then, is subjective. By our nature, we are disposed to accumulate resources without limit, to dominate others and to live in constant fear. In describing the state of nature as a state of war of all against all, Hobbes emphasized the subjective side. But objective and subjective circumstances work together to render the state of nature dire. If we were much more unequal in natural endowments, or if we could avoid contact with one another, or if nature more nearly resembled a lifeboat with insufficient supplies for all (absolute scarcity) or the plentitude of the Garden of Eden (abundance), the terms of human interaction in the absence of a sovereign would be radically different, regardless of our inherent dispositions. Likewise, if our dispositions were different — if, say we were content to do without even to the point of extinction, or if we had no interest in dominating others and not subordinating ourselves, or if we were reckless and unconcerned with our lives and well being — the state of nature, its objective conditions given, would not be the same war of all against all Hobbes described.

Hobbes's state of nature is eternal — holding for all human beings, in all circumstances, at all times — but for the 'solution' provided by the institution of sovereignty. Hobbes conceived human nature and the human condition ahistorically.

Objective and subjective conditions work together to produce the war of all against all, but it is human nature that Hobbes privileged. Only an ahistorical view of human nature permits this representation. Even supposing Hobbes right, it would still be possible to imagine circumstances capable of neutralizing the eternal propensity for competition and conflict. Such beings as Hobbes thought we are would live in peace in the Garden of Eden. But so long as war is inscribed in our nature, the state of war, as a generalized disposition, will always be with us — even if circumstances should somehow combine to promote peace. The state of war can be benign, but it cannot be evaded.[2]

Rousseau took over Hobbes's description of the state of nature, but historicized Hobbes's account of its subjective component. For Rousseau,[3] human beings are not egoists by nature but through the force of what Marx would call social relations of production. What exists trans-historically is the disposition we share with other animals to be guided by self-concern (*amour de soi*) and a primitive capacity for empathic sociability or pity (*pitié*), also shared at least with higher animals. It is the effect of private property upon these innate dispositions that makes *amour propre*, Hobbesian egoism, the principle that directs our actions.[4] If Rousseau is right, the Hobbesian state of nature, insofar as it depends on human nature being as Hobbes thought, is, *pace* Hobbes, historically produced.

Rousseau did not expressly draw this conclusion because his account of the dependence of human nature on real property relations is not, strictly, historical. Rousseau recognized variability, but not historicity. However the idea that *amour propre* is an effect of private property is plainly amenable to an historical materialist reconstruction.[5] Human nature is not just variable, but historically variable depending, as Rousseau thought, on real property relations, and therefore ultimately, as Rousseau never imagined, on the level of development of productive forces. In denying that Hobbes's account of human nature holds regardless of circumstances, Rousseau suggested, to those who would read him after Marx, that Hobbes's account be historicized; and that the privileged role Hobbes accorded human nature be abandoned in favour of a theory of historically developing objective conditions.

The component of the received view that an historical materialist reconstruction of the fundamental problem renders most problematic is, of course, relative scarcity. Hobbes and Rousseau take it as given that nature is sufficiently abundant to render cooperation rational, and sufficiently niggardly to make it necessary. However these parameters are imprecise. In some sense, relative scarcity is a trans-historical fact. It is conceivable, though unlikely, that most of what we want could become absolutely scarce — rendering cooperation irrational. However it is much more likely, as Marx maintained, that, barring exogenous interferences, means for satisfying human wants will increase. Some goods will always be scarce in virtue of the cost of producing them in abundance; and there are some goods whose value depends on being rare. In addition, it will always be necessary for individuals to budget — and ration — allocations of time. But to acknowledge the inexorability of (relative) scarcity is not to deny that there can be changes in degrees of scarcity relevant for imaginary reconstructions of human life in the absence of states. Indeed, after Marx, ahistorical accounts of the objective conditions human beings confront are eminently indefensible.

Rousseau, like Hobbes before him, identified the state's foundation with its origin; not by directly confounding an historical hypothesis with a justifying theory, but in a more subtle and revealing way. Rousseau depicted statelessness as a pre-political and primitive condition. His state of nature is abstracted from and prior to actual history, a history that includes, among other things, states and the benefits states have provided for moral and material development. In effect, Rousseau identified statelessness at the beginning of history with statelessness 'under the aspect of eternity'. The state he proposed as the solution to the fundamental problem of political life is therefore 'a form of association' that, though eternal, is also radically new in relation to the state of nature that precedes it. Historical materialism blocks this understanding. To conceive a state of nature from an historical materialist perspective is to imagine statelessness at a determinate moment in a specifiable trajectory. Rousseau's imaginary pre-political condition is, in other words, only one among many states of nature.

In part, Rousseau's depiction of the state of nature is an artifact of contractarian methodology. It is also a consequence of his search for eternal and unchanging forms. The *de jure* state is a first state because it is an ideal state — a timeless reality, standing apart from history and its vicissitudes. Origins in fact and foundations in right are, of course, distinct. But the contractarian method requires that the state's foundation be depicted as an originating act; that the state succeed the state of nature in time. Though the state the social contract founds is eternal, the contract upon which it is based is not. Contracts are initiated at particular moments, after a period when they were not yet in force. Thus the state of nature precedes the *de jure* state temporally, at the same time that it underlies it logically; a patent equivocation that is unavoidable so long as the intent is to conceive an eternal, notional entity by contractarian means.

The story cannot be told otherwise. The ambiguity is inscribed in the project.

Historical materialism opposes Rousseau's foundational project and therefore also his depiction of the social contract as an originating act. In the historical materialist scheme, the state is not a notional entity in a Platonic universe, an eternal reality grounding authority claims *de jure.* The state just is what it is *de facto*: an ever-changing adaptation to a developing historical reality. The search for foundations in right is misguided, not because political superstructures are somehow epiphenomenal on modes of production, but because the state itself is not a pure idea, permanent and intelligible apart from its historical role. For Marx, states are essentially historical entities, existing in real time, not in a timeless noumenal order; and their time in the flux of historical change is anything but permanent.

But the idea of a state of nature — of human life in the absence of states — can survive the abandonment of Rousseau's justificatory objectives. The state of nature can even be employed within an historical materialist framework to great advantage. In what follows here, it will be taken as established, after all that has been argued, that Rousseau's 'fundamental problem' should be recast to accord with historical materialism's view of the state's role in actual history. Accordingly, the state of nature will be employed here as a device for thinking about states as solutions to a problem whose terms change as productive forces develop.

Solutions

Socialism and therefore communism depend on the massive development of productive forces; a level of development vastly exceeding what Rousseau imagined for the state of nature. Even very high levels of development will not undo all material bases for competition over resources. But the level of development prerequisite for socialism does radically alter the terms of competition and also its stakes. A 'socialist state of nature' — corresponding to the level of development necessary for socialism — differs qualitatively from the state of nature that motivated Rousseau's social contract. And it has very different implications for the state that follows it.

The fundamental problem of political life is, in effect, to

coordinate individuals' behaviour to accord with their fundamental interests. For Hobbes, the point was to secure peace and avoid the war of all against all. For Rousseau, autonomy was overwhelmingly the most important interest for political institutions to protect and foster. The difference is far-reaching, as we have seen; but at the level of abstraction appropriate for contriving solutions to the problem they each posed, it can be ignored. What matters is how interests are addressed; not what they are.

As mentioned in Chapter 7, Hobbes and Rousseau after him thought fundamental interests jeopardized in the state of nature for a reason that can be made perspicuous in 'game' theoretic terms. In a state of nature, individuals confront a generalized Prisoners' Dilemma: a 'game' where dominant strategies produce sub-optimal outcomes. In Prisoners' Dilemma situations, by doing better for ourselves individually, we actually do worse for ourselves than we otherwise might.

Suppose, for the sake of illustration, that there are only two players, A and B, and that they each have two possible moves: either player can 'cooperate' (say, by conforming to rules that regulate competition between them) or 'defect' (by disregarding these rules). Imagine, then, the following pay-off structure. A's pay-offs are written on the left; B's on the right:

		B's moves	
		cooperate	defect
A's moves	cooperate	1,1	−2,2
	defect	2,−2	−1,−1

If both A and B cooperate, each gets a pay-off of 1; if both defect, each gets −1. If one cooperates and the other defects, the defector gets a pay-off of 2; while the cooperator gets −2. Assuming A and B are rationally self-interested, they will each defect. A will reason as follows: 'My pay-off depends on what B does. B will either defect or cooperate. If B defects, I should defect too, since −1 is better than −2. However if B cooperates, I should also defect, since 2 is better than 1. In other words, whatever B does, I am better off defecting.' Since the pay-offs B confronts are exactly symmetrical, B will reason similarly. Therefore both will defect and the outcome will be −1 for each. But they could have done better had they cooperated. The socially optimal outcome, 1,1, is eluded if the players do what is in their best interests individually.[6]

Hobbes's and Rousseau's states of nature are generalized Prisoners' Dilemmas because the conditions they stipulate are such that, in general, cooperation — conformity to rules requiring individuals sometimes to forbear from maximizing pay-offs to themselves — is necessary for outcomes to be optimal, but defection is always the dominant strategy.[7] For each individual, cooperation is irrational. However individuals would be better off cooperating i.e. 'better off' in the sense that it is rational for them to defect. In a state of nature, then, individuals do less well than they otherwise might. But insofar as they are rational maximizers, they cannot do otherwise. Agreements to achieve better net outcomes through cooperation will never be stable because, for each individual, there is a rationally compelling incentive to defect. Agreement cannot end the state of nature.

Prisoners' Dilemmas admit of a variety of solutions, of varying degrees of appropriateness, depending upon the particularities of the pay-off structure and the degree of intransigent self-interestedness imputed to the players of the game. In addition to political solutions that invoke external coordination, psychological solutions are conceivable. In general, political solutions change the pay-off structures that define the game; psychological solutions change the dispositions of the parties confronting these pay-offs. Mixed solutions are also imaginable.

If relative scarcity somehow ceased to pertain or if individuals were not rational maximizers, the state of nature would not be a Prisoners' Dilemma. Hobbes thought the objective and subjective conditions he imputed to the state of nature immutable. Rousseau denied the immutability of human nature, at the same time that he affirmed the inevitability of Hobbes's account of it once private property has been successfully introduced. Historical materialism challenges these understandings radically, but not so radically as to deny the conditions that make a state of nature a Prisoners' Dilemma. After Marx, we can imagine statelessness in a world where relative scarcity and even individual rationality (in a sense consonant with Hobbes's and Rousseau's view) hold, but where solutions different from Hobbes's and Rousseau's are conceivable and even likely.

In principle, sub-optimal outcomes could be avoided if defection were somehow made impossible. But this solution is not feasible for the full range of behaviour requiring coordination in a state of nature. Defection generally cannot be precluded by physical restraints, and neither is there any other way to make it impossible. But what cannot be achieved directly can be approximated indirectly. Hobbes's idea, endorsed by Rousseau, is to change the pay-off structure individuals confront by contriving a means for imposing sanctions on defectors. Despite all that distinguishes Hobbes's and Rousseau's respective views of the state and the social contract that establishes it, they agree that states organize cooperation by instituting and enforcing rules. In essence, sovereignty, the state in its 'active' aspect,[8] is a device for ensuring coordination; for doing what individuals in a state of nature cannot accomplish by agreement alone.

But if classes truly play the role they are assigned by Marx, and if the state does organize class domination, Hobbes's and Rousseau's characterization of 'the fundamental problem' cannot be sustained in general and, of course, neither can their respective solutions. In failing to recognize the reality of social classes and the role of political institutions in class struggle, they failed to recognize the constitutive role of classes in political institutions. They therefore misrepresented an intra-class coordination problem as a generalized, inter-individual problem.[9] But ironically, communism — a possible outcome (indeed, in the orthodox view, an inevitable outcome) of the long history of classes and their struggles — would make Hobbes and Rousseau right. Obviously, in a classless society, the fundamental coordination problem could no longer be at an intra-class level. Insofar as a generalized Prisoners' Dilemma remains, it could only be a problem for individuals. But where communism is possible, materially and institutionally, the state of nature would no longer be the state of nature Hobbes and Rousseau imagined. For communism supposes, first, vast societal wealth (approaching generalized abundance) and, above all, the radical transformation of human nature, away from *amour propre* towards the generality of the will.

The transformation in human beings required for communism is, of course, psychological. People must become more communal and more inclined to subordinate private to general interests. In Rousseau's and Robespierre's sense, they must become more 'virtuous'. Or, in the sense Rousseau anticipated and Kant made explicit, they must become more moral; more inclined to assess alternative courses of action as pure personalities adopting the standpoint of generality, not empirically distinct selves bent on improving their own positions. Moral solutions to Prisoners' Dilemmas are a subset of psychological solutions generally. It is worth noting a few other solutions or partial solutions, if only to appreciate better how much of human nature must be transformed for moral solutions to work.

One solution would be for individuals to become more trustworthy out of plain self-interest. Geographical proximity is an important, if unstated, objective condition supposed in standard, contractarian accounts of the state of nature: individuals cannot avoid repeated interactions.[10] Thus the same players will repeat Prisoners' Dilemma games indefinitely many times. Defection is a dominant strategy if the game is not repeated. But when the game is continually replayed, players who employ cooperative strategies will generally do better than those who do not. Cooperative strategies will therefore be selected (in the way that Darwin hypothesized selection for fitness); and trustworthiness will evolve.[11] In principle, then, individuals should become capable of coordinating their behaviour without recourse to political constraints. It is moot, however, how trustworthy individuals can become and it is unlikely, so long as private interests remain preeminent, that states could become entirely superfluous through this route. Arguably, Hobbes — and Rousseau after him — over-emphasized the need for states by under-estimating individuals' capacities for evolving cooperative strategies. Then the state of nature would not be quite the war of all against all they supposed. But so long as defection remains an overriding temptation, coercive force will be required to suppress its inevitable eruptions. It will also be helpful in bolstering the morale of cooperators by assuring them that, in cooperating, they are not being duped. Arguably, individuals moved by private interests will always require such assurance, if they are to cooperate voluntarily.

Liberals have long pointed out that opinion and other forms of social pressure can function coercively. But public opinion can also shape motivational structures psychologically. It can instil dispositions against 'free riding'. Defectors are free-riders. By not cooperating, they seek to do as well for themselves as they can, while others contribute to outcomes from which they benefit. It may be that, in the final analysis, states are indispensable for forcing free-riders to cooperate. But social pressure surely contributes; and not just in its coercive aspects. It motivates cooperation.

In general, any psychological change that overwhelms the egoistic motivations that prompt defection can solve Prisoners' Dilemmas in principle. If players prefer to cooperate, cooperation, not defection, becomes the rational strategy. However, so long as private interest remains in force, the temptation to defect will persist. It can be countered but, in general, it cannot be overwhelmed. A political solution will therefore be unavoidable. To be sure, no association can hold together for long only through force. A disposition to cooperate, however inculcated and sustained, is indispensable. But failing the realization of a general will, there is no substitute for states. In the final analysis, only the use or threat of force permits a sure and definitive escape from the state of nature.

However the moral solution, if universally adopted, would end the regime of private interest and therefore, in principle, the need for a state. If each player does only what would be rationally willed for all players, no one could adopt a strategy enjoining defection. For defection, by hypothesis, produces less than ideal outcomes; and no one could will that outcomes be worse than they might otherwise be. The point is not that in a Prisoners' Dilemma everyone wants everyone else to cooperate. That desire is eminently self-interested. The idea, instead, is that cooperation is enjoined for rational agents assessing alternatives impersonally. So long as deliberation proceeds from the standpoint of generality, cooperation will result. Insofar as Kant, following Rousseau, was right to insist that reason itself requires this standpoint, then reason moves us from the state of nature to a republic of ends.

Diminishing Scarcity/Increasing Rationality

Communist societies would, of course, operate on different principles from preceding social orders, with far-reaching implications for political institutions. It is easy, however, to overstate the changes communism would entail and Marxists, including Marx, have readily succumbed to the temptation. In reflecting on the implications of communism for the future of the state, it is important therefore to exercise caution and not claim more than can be plausibly supported.

Eliminating classes is not tantamount to removing social discord. There is no reason to expect coordination problems to resolve themselves automatically in the absence of class divisions. Communism implies the end of the state only if the state is defined by what it does in class societies. Then, under communism, the state would end by definition. However, proponents of the traditional doctrine intend more; though precisely what they intend is unclear. If the claim is that (*de facto*) legitimate, institutionalized violence 'withers away' completely, the position cannot be sustained. Communism would likely diminish the need for coordination through force, but not eliminate it entirely. Under communism, however, institutionalized violence would cease to be the basis of political association. If Marx was right, existing states in class societies are based on force. State power constitutes a collective will in the interest of the economically dominant class. Under communism, the state in this sense does indeed end. In communist societies, the collective will is neither heteronomously determined nor imposed by force. As in the *de jure* state, the collective will is the freely determined will of each constitutent member.

The idea that all antagonistic social divisions disappear with the end of class society is facile and unsustainable, but not wrong-headed. Though ending class divisions would not eliminate societal discord (except discord arising from class divisions), there is reason to hold that the conditions necessary for ending class divisions would mitigate societal discord severely. The diminishing scarcity that makes socialism (and, at a later stage, communism) materially possible and the transformations in human nature required for communism to be politically feasible make a moral solution to the Prisoners' Dilemma problem Hobbes and Rousseau identified tenable.

Rousseau acknowledged the dangers posed to the general will by class divisions only implicitly, but he expressly forbade gross inequalities of income and wealth, stipulating that 'none should be so rich as to be able to buy another; and none so poor as to be forced to sell himself'.[12] Material inequalities foster a consciousness of difference that detracts from solidarity — making prospects for 'the exercise of the general will' remote. So long as resources remain relatively scarce, distributional questions will be paramount; and egalitarian distributions will be instrumental for forming individuals capable of becoming indivisible parts of the sovereign — not just notionally, but in fact. Once development surpasses the threshold beyond which communism becomes materially possible, however, distributional questions will pale in importance. Where there is massive wealth, justice will matter less than it does at lower levels of development. In short, the material conditions for communism diminish the importance of justice, and *a fortiori* of egalitarian distributions. What Rousseau would achieve by limiting inequalities is achieved alternatively by augmenting productivity to the point where distributional considerations matter qualitively less.

In the earliest state of nature recounted in *The Second Discourse*, individuals made few demands on nature. Population was sparse enough and nature sufficiently generous to supply virtually all the demands the primitive mind could contrive. In this primordial condition, human beings confronted abundance. To be sure, there was less wealth than in subsequent periods, but nearly everything that was desired could be obtained with little effort and at no cost to anyone else. There was no competition for resources; and therefore no question of justice. Rousseau never quite imagined the reemergence of this fortunate condition at a higher stage of development. The first state of nature was a Golden Age, never to be recovered. But the mythical abundance Rousseau imagined — though at a vastly higher level of development — is precisely what historical materialism deems possible. Development produces (relative) scarcity and then finally overcomes scarcity — recovering abundance, as it were, at a higher level.

Or nearly so. Abundance can only be approximated as a limit. It may therefore be impossible ever entirely to move 'beyond justice' by superseding the conditions under which justice matters. But, if Marx was right, it is possible to cross a threshold beyond which distributive justice becomes only a marginal consideration in human affairs. Thus Marx discounted the importance of justice under communism, while acknowledging the persistence of distributional concerns. He insisted that, under communism, distributions would proceed: 'from each according to ability, to each according to need'.[13] Evidently, this principle was intended descriptively as an account of the structure of distributions in a world where the circumstances of justice have effectively (though not entirely) ceased to apply.[14] Distribution according to need is not quite distribution according to wants. Wants can be boundless, taxing even the most developed productive forces beyond their capacity. Needs, insofar as they can be distinguished from wants, are less demanding even if, as Marx thought, needs expand with the development of productive capacities. In Marx's view, communist societies can and will distribute according to need: individuals will satisfy needs from a common stock provided by all who are able to contribute. 'To each according to wants' envisages a society literally 'beyond justice'. The communism Marx imagined falls short of this vision. But it is as near an approximation as human beings can expect.

The degree of scarcity obtaining at a given time depends, of course, on the level of development of productive forces and the bountifulness of nature. But what matters most are the demands individuals make upon the circumstances they confront. If demands are few, as in Rousseau's first state of nature, scarcity can be nearly overcome with hardly any development at all and with only a normally bountiful nature. Motivational structures, therefore, are crucial. So long as *amour propre* persists, there will be scarcity, no matter how massively developed productive forces become. Thus abundance supposes the end of rational egoism or, to maintain the Hegelian idiom that here seems appropriate, the restoration — at a higher stage — of *amour de soi.* In Rousseau's scheme, humanity passes from self-concern, through rational egoism, to full essential humanity — through the exercise of the general will. But it is only after *amour propre* has transformed human beings and the world they confront that non-acquisitive self-concern, directed towards 'the whole community', again becomes possible.

It is unnecessary here to elaborate the complex principles of Kantian moral philosophy or to rehearse the obscure arguments that led Kant to the idea of a republic of ends. It is important to recall, however, a feature of Kantian theory that distinguishes it from other positions in moral philosophy and, at the same time, gives the republic of ends a determinate political content. In doing so, it should be remembered that Kant proposed the republic of ends as a metaphor for the moral order he envisaged, not as a political objective. There are reasons though for according the republic of ends a more literal interpretation than its inventor intended.

In Kant's view, reason rules on the content of persons' ends negatively — by proscribing 'maxims' (principles of action) that fail to satisfy the categorical imperative. Only maxims that are universal are warranted for rational agents. However to will only what can be willed by any rational agent is, Kant argued, to treat the capacity for rational determination — in oneself and in others — as an end in itself. The categorical imperative is therefore equivalent, in Kant's view, to (absolute) respect for the autonomy of persons as bearers of rational wills. Thus rationality does not individuate: whatever is binding on one rational agent is binding on any other rational agent similarly circumstanced; and whatever is binding without qualification and regardless of circumstances is binding on all. Kant maintained that the categorical imperative picks out a set of principles of this sort. These objective principles of action are moral laws. Moral laws, then, are not imposed from without — by God or nature. They are constituted autonomously, by ourselves insofar as we are rational. They are 'objective' in the sense that they hold for any and all rational agents, but they bind in virtue of their being self-prescribed. Conformity to the moral law therefore is autonomy: determination by a law of one's own legislation.

If moral laws were imposed from without, order could be achieved through subordination to moral laws provided, of course, they are consistent and sufficiently encompassing to regulate individuals' activities satisfactorily. However the burden of Kant's practical philosophy was to show how moral order lies within; how the universal and non-individuating character of practical reason suffices to generate a 'harmony of rational wills'. The novelty of Kant's vision is encoded in this formulation. Order is intrinsic to rational willing, and therefore autonomously constituted. In alternative visions, order is conceivable, but at the cost of autonomy, through subordination to a will distinct from one's own. However for Kant as for Rousseau, autonomy is literally all that matters; it is the source and condition of value. Thus Kant follows Rousseau in maintaining that, in the final analysis, morality is a property of communities; specifically, of the community of rational agents. The political metaphor, the republic of ends, is therefore appropriate. Unlike existing states, the republic of ends is not based upon force. But, like all states, it is a polity, a community of persons drawn together for a common end.

As Rousseau had already shown, the republic of ends is not a substantive system of laws, but an organization of persons (conceived as bearers of rational wills) for making laws. In short, it is a Rousseauean democracy, a 'legislature' that discovers the general will. The laws this 'moral and collective body' enacts are self-legislated; and the order that results is constituted collectively in consequence of mutual and absolute respect for autonomy in oneself and others. Where reason is not entirely in control, the Kantian ideal is approximated in institutions that make collective choices through majority rule voting or other democratic procedures such as the direct democratic assemblies envisaged in *The Social Contract* or more remote approximations necessitated by circumstance.[15] The republic of ends is the regulative principle towards which radical democratic institutions tend. It is the 'end' of the dictatorship of the proletariat.

Rousseau may have been right in supposing that this regulative idea can never be realized entirely 'taking men as they are'. But there is reason to think he was also right to insist that with 'laws as they might be made', human nature can change. After Marx, we can view the reconstruction of laws or, more generally, the creation and transformation of political institutions, as a sustained historical process; one that, under socialism, can be consciously undertaken and directed. The republic of ends can therefore become a deliberate political objective.

The Republic of Ends on Earth

Marx was reluctant to speculate on the shape of things to come except in very general terms. Officially, he wanted to distinguish scientific socialism, based on a theory of history and 'the laws of motion' of capitalist societies, from utopian socialisms, based only on visions of ideal institutional arrangements. It is also evident that those elements of Marxian theory that support the idea of communism — historical materialism and the strain of political theory that joins Rousseauean themes — do not help much in filling in details. Except in their broadest contours, the institutional features of communist societies will depend on the historical, geographical and conjunctural concerns important to Tocqueville and Burke and prominent also in the non-Kantian strain of Rousseau's political philosophy.

Similar considerations apply even to the dictatorship of the proletariat though with diminished consequence, inasmuch as the socialist state, even in this virtually unprecedented and utterly unfamiliar form, is closer to our own experience than is its 'end'. We can say with assurance that in socialist states leading to communism, direct democratic decision-making would, so far as possible, replace representative government, and democratic rule would be extended into economic decision-making and throughout society. We can therefore conclude that the received distinction between politics and society (including the economy) would no longer obtain, and that the state would progressively merge into a politicized and democratized 'civil society'.[16] Precise specifications cannot be provided at this level of abstraction; and a salutary conservatism, reduced to its rational kernel, should brace us against the attempt. But since radical democratization does have evident implications, there is more to be said nevertheless.

In *The State and Revolution*, Lenin emphasized implications of the envisaged extension of democratic rule that require dismantling the distinctive institutional arrangements of capitalist states and their replacement by institutions of a different sort. It is not necessary to elaborate details of the particular measures Lenin proposed, but it is worthwhile to reflect on the principle that underlies his proposals. If the republic of ends truly is the destination of the transformative process the dictatorship of the proletariat directs, its institutional features, so far as they are conceivable from our vantage-point, will be best appreciated by extrapolating from what can be said with somewhat greater confidence about proletarian class rule.

Of course, the dictatorship of the proletariat is problematic even as an ideal.[17] Arguably, the Bolshevik Revolution established a proletarian class dictatorship. There are few today though who would promote Soviet political institutions — even in their pristine, pre-Stalinist form — as models to be emulated. The dictatorship of the proletariat in its 'normal form' is vastly more attractive, but many would hesitate to endorse it too. Radical democracy for direct producers and their allies can threaten the values liberals aim to protect when they assert claims for individuals' rights or proscribe state (and societal) interferences with specified activities. Proletarian democracy threatens to unleash 'the tyranny of the majority' against former exploiters but also against members of the majority itself. Insofar as the republic of ends is the end-point or limiting case of proletarian class dictatorship, questions can also be raised about its desirability. It will be well briefly to address these hesitations by reflecting further on democratic statelessness as an ideal.

Proletarian class dictatorships, according to Lenin, develop a state apparatus uniquely suited to popular participation and control. Since, in Lenin's view, state institutions exist mainly to repress — to use or threaten force — his focus centered on what he called 'the repressive state apparatus', and he represented the dictatorship of the proletariat, accordingly, as a repressive state apparatus of a new type. All capitalist societies, even those with dictatorial (as opposed to representative) governments, have specialized and (relatively) independent institutions for ensuring order: police, para-military police and the military itself. Moreover all capitalist societies have a relatively independent system for 'the administration of justice'. In *The State and Revolution*, Lenin proposed replacing the former with popular militias, the people in arms, and the latter with popular tribunals. Just as representative government gives way to direct democratic rule (or some feasible approximation), the repressive apparatus of capitalist states give way to a repressive apparatus in which the people themselves exercise control directly.

There is good reason to be wary of popular control, however, and it is not for nothing that liberals have endeavoured persistently to justify restricting its scope. Were the repressive state apparatus to lose its (relatively) independent character, it would lose the benefits of functionaries' expertise, while becoming liable to the vicissitudes of popular sentiment. The dictatorship of the proletariat evidently risks this consequence. A separate police and army are, by all accounts, more 'professional' than a popular militia and, despite all the abuses to which they are prone, more inclined to respect the rights of the policed. Similarly, a popular tribunal is far less likely than an independent court to conduct its business according to proper legal standards or to respect the rights of unpopular defendants. If, at the limit, there ceased to be any specialized instruments of repression at all — if the repressive state apparatus as such withered away — the result, apparently, would be unrestrained vigilantism. But a world where vigilantes roam free is hardly ideal. It is a Hobbesian state of nature resurrected.

Communists, of course, want a republic of ends, not a Hobbesian state of nature, and it would be the bitterest of historical ironies if the former were to degenerate into the latter at the end of history. What stands in the way is just the historical materialist case for development and its beneficial consequences and, above all, faith in the potentialities of human nature transformed through democratic participation at all levels of social, economic and political life. The republic of ends is not a Hobbesian state of nature because its citizens are not rational egoists confronting relative scarcity. They are rational (Kantian) persons in a world of near abundance.

In the final analysis, then, the desirability of communist statelessness — and of the dictatorship of the proletariat that brings it to fruition — depends on the efficacy of democracy itself in transforming human nature. Democracy creates the conditions for its own desirability and, at the limit, for transcending the state altogether. Political theory cannot definitively vindicate this claim. It calls for empirical corroboration and, where possible, historical support. Inasmuch as all the evidence is by no means in and the bearing of the pertinent available data is disputable, commitment to democracy can only be a kind of wager. At this remove from real history and politics, the most that can be shown is that, in view of the stakes, the wager is reasonable.[18]

So long as history remains the history of class struggles, an interest in intra-class cooperation and inter-class conflict will exist. There will therefore always be a material basis for societal discord. With the end of class struggle, this condition will disappear. If Marx was right, there are no other material impediments to internal coordination, beyond scarcity itself (to the extent it continues to pertain). Discord in Rousseau's state of nature was generally self-defeating. Development renders it increasingly irrational. It may be that, even with (virtual) abundance, human nature is such that (irrational) discord is unavoidable, and the need for external coordination insurmountable. Then even if communism were achieved, the need for force would remain. Some specialized and perhaps even some (relatively) independent apparatus for coordinating behaviour coercively may therefore always be with us, even if humanity advances as far as is materially and institutionally possible. The explanation would lie precisely where Rousseau thought: with human beings' incapacity, even in the most propitious circumstances, to realize autonomy fully.

Communist statelessness accords fully with the classical picture of human beings as political animals. The end of the state yields a social order where individuals devote their lives to public deliberation and debate and even collective choice. This conclusion would seem paradoxical, were we not accustomed by now to the appropriateness of the Hegelian image of self-transcendence. In superseding itself, a stateless society incorporates features of the state it 'negates'. Not everyone will find this vision attractive. Many of us would dread the prospect of a life spent in meetings and the 'squandering' of energy and time in public pursuits. This prospect probably would be dreadful in a social order where private interest reigned. Then participation might even facilitate the domination of some individuals by others, impeding autonomy and obstructing full and equal membership in an earthly republic of ends. But communism supposes an order where private interest is overcome, and Rousseau's ideal of an internally coordinated association of persons — grounded in each individual's essential autonomy — is finally realized. In this genuine 'republic of virtue', the classical ideal would take on a different cast.

With equality of moral personality assured, human beings, expressing their natures freely, would stand revealed as the political animals they are and the apolitical life would seem not worth living. Or so Rousseau and a host of others have thought. I share their expectation. However I still suspect that this vision will not appeal universally to people formed in prevailing, liberal institutions. A life dedicated to citizenship in Rousseau's sense is not a continuation of what is attractive in liberalism. It offends the Augustinian sense of politics as an affliction. Socialism generally realizes liberal values better than capitalism, its historical rival.[19] But socialism's 'final stage', communism — the possible issue of a protracted revolutionary struggle in and over the state — is more remote from prevailing standards. Communism is not a new epoch in the historical materialist sense, but it is a new age in the history of human freedom and a radical break with forms of life and therefore forms of consciousness developed in class societies. Even from this distance, however, I think many of us can recognize the appeal of the classical vision, finally democratized under communist conditions, and its manifest superiority to alternative arrangements that we might nevertheless prefer for ourselves.

In Engels's celebrated expression (and in Saint-Simon's before him), under communism, 'the governance of men' gives way to 'the administration of things'. Thus even classical Marxism never quite claimed that communism would be entirely without a centralized, coordinating apparatus, but only that this apparatus would 'administer' rather than 'govern'. It is not clear what difference these words intend. Ostensibly what was envisaged were non-coercive institutions for coordinating economic and social life. Of course, nothing more concrete was specified and, lacking the gift of prophecy, it is likely nothing more could be. The notion is intriguing, but mysterious. It must remain so here.

To be sure, the question of the nature of administration under communism — and the related question of the individuation of political entities and their articulation — cannot be evaded forever.[20] If these 'practical' problems cannot be solved, the vision that ultimately requires their solution cannot be sustained. I would hazard that these problems can be solved but only, as it were, in process — in the course of constructing communism. At the level of abstraction appropriate for assessing the cogency of the communist (and anarchist) vision, nothing more can be said than that practitioners of a genuinely communist politics must expect to be able to muddle through. In speculating on the institutional arrangements of the future, Tocqueville's and Burke's distrust of theory seems eminently wise. If it is an evasion to relegate the issue of implementation to future practice, it is at least a deliberate evasion, warranted by conservative good sense.

It should be noted, however, that like so many other important notions of classical Marxian theory, the administration of things too has precedent in Rousseau's political philosophy. For Rousseau, private interests threaten the exercise of the general will, and institutions that mediate between the individual and the state always generate private interests. It is therefore necessary that partial institutions be proscribed.[21] But sovereignty requires a means for its execution, a government; government is, of course, a partial institution, standing between the individual and the state. The burden of *The Social Contract*, Book III is to square this circle: to show how governments can execute the sovereign's will without usurping sovereignty itself. As could have been predicted, the attempt is only partially successful.[22] But the problem is unavoidable. Even where there is a consensus on ends, actually as well as notionally, there is need for means to implement the consensus, to execute the general will.

Institutions that administer without governing are, in effect, Rousseauean 'governments' — in circumstances where the material and psychological prerequisites for communism exist. Since a consensus on ends can then be assumed, 'things' can be administered without governance, though not necessarily without force. What everyone truly wants can somehow simply be done. This claim is vague and unhelpful. 'The administration of things' is a place-holder expression; not a description of institutional arrangements. It is a name for what cannot be theorized in the absence of an appropriate practice to reflect upon. Rousseau effectively formulated the problem and Engels, following Saint-Simon, changed its terms evocatively. In doing so, Engels reached the limits of what can be plausibly maintained. The result is meagre and unsatisfying, but unavoidable and wise. In this case, there *is* virtue in necessity. To attempt more would be to risk the temptations of utopian theorizing; with the dire implications conservative critics have cogently warned against.

Conclusion

States are 'grounded' in force in the sense that, by definition, they are coercive: they coordinate behaviour through the use or threat of force. I have argued that states are indeed necessary for solving coordination problems, so long as material conditions fall short of abundance and persons are not yet educated to full democratic citizenship in Rousseau's sense. I have also argued that, in principle, economic growth (rationally deployed) and radical democracy can undo the conditions that make states necessary. We have seen, however, that in class societies, force plays yet another, more insidious role: it exacerbates coordination problems for subordinate and potentially insurgent classes. Thus the capitalist state solves the coordination problem capitalists face, the better to decapacitate the workers capitalists exploit. The socialist state, in contrast, *can* help solve the coordination problem workers confront; but only if it is democratized, the better to decapacitate former and potential exploiters. In the Marxian view, which I have endorsed, the end of the state comes when this divisive use of force finally withers away for want of subordinate classes to suppress. I have argued that the same process leads to the virtual elimination of public uses of force, even for facilitating cooperation. Under socialist and democratic conditions, the exercise of the general will can progressively replace force. In this sense, the state can end, and be replaced by a republic of ends. It is likely, as Rousseau thought, that this process can never be realized perfectly. Then, in consequence of human recalcitrance, even republics of ends might still use force. But insofar as full democratic equality is achieved, human communities, for the first time since the emergence of classes, would no longer be grounded in force. The end of the state would be achieved.

Is the end of the state, the goal of communists and anarchists, feasible? I have argued that an affirmative answer is plausible, on condition that:

(1) capitalism is replaced by socialism or, equivalently, exploitation based on capitalist property relations ends; and
(2) a socialist state is established and maintained that directs its policies expressly towards creating a communist (and stateless) future. This state would be permanently revolutionary, permanently opposed to the interests of the beneficiaries of forms of exploitation that survive the transition from capitalism to socialism.

The possibility of satisfying (1) is well supported by historical materialism and, of course, by actual history. (2) is supported by defensible positions in political theory. The claims I have advanced in support of (2) are strongly linked, historically and conceptually, with Rousseauean and Marxian views on politics. But it has generally not been possible to endorse their actual positions without substantial alterations. Similarly, the theory of history I have appealed to is not exactly the theory Marx proposed, though it does retain many of the substantive positions of orthodox historical materialism and all of its conceptually distinctive features.

The Marxian name for the type of state proposed in (2) is the dictatorship of the proletariat. The name has misled advocates and opponents from its inception. By developing a more general theory of the socialist state than classical Marxism advanced, we have seen that the dictatorship of the proletariat does have a defensible rational kernel, after all. As argued, the normal form of the dictatorship of the proletariat is radical democracy for the overwhelming majority; popular control over political, social and economic institutions. I have held that democracy is indispensable not only for governance in socialist societies in transition to communism, but also for the education of socialists. Communism requires substantial modifications in human beings' dispositions and character; changes it is reasonable (though far from certain) to expect democratization to promote.

I have maintained, finally, that the republic of ends, the end of the state, is the limiting case or end-point of proletarian class dictatorship. Its institutional features cannot be prophesied in detail, but it is clear that communism would extend and deepen democracy. It is also likely that communism could not dispense entirely with a centralized, directing and, if need be, coercive apparatus — for 'the administration of things' and to overcome collective weaknesses of will. Rousseau was therefore right to point to the inexorable impediments raised by human nature itself. But in emphasizing the coercive aspect of the *de jure* state, Rousseau exaggerated the extent of human recalcitrance, even implying that a radical diminution of coordination through force is a utopian dream. Rousseau's failing was that he was not an historical materialist. After Marx, there is reason to think that internal coordination is indeed on the historical agenda and can be closely approximated; that coordination through force can wither away (almost) to nothing.

Is this vision desirable? Certainly not if human nature remains untransformed. The dictatorship of the proletariat would then be a tyranny of the majority and, at the limit, communism would devolve into a Hobbesian state of nature. The burden of the communist vision therefore depends on the beneficial, transformative effects of the dictatorship of the proletariat. I have argued that commitment to this ideal depends, in the end, on faith in democracy. This faith has deep roots in our political culture and its theory. It has long sustained progressive and revolutionary politics. In the face of the retrogressive and anti-democratic politics that has come into prominence in all the major liberal democracies, it is crucial that this longstanding commitment be revived and deepened. Rosa Luxemburg long ago identified the alternative as barbarism. Today it is clear that predictions of barbarism are optimistic; that annihilating nuclear war is a much more likely outcome of politics as usual. I submit that communism — the most radical imaginable democratic empowerment — is, in the long run, the only feasible alternative to this eventuality.

For conservatives like Tocqueville and Burke, revolutionary ventures are nearly always ill-conceived. Tradition, circumstance and conjuncture work together to ensure that positive change can occur only if it is pursued gradually and piecemeal.

Robespierre and his fellow Jacobins had just the contrary sense. Each tendency of thought bears strong conceptual affinities with Rousseauean political philosophy, and each is insightful and important. Revolutionaries do need to appropriate Tocqueville's and Burke's attention to tradition, circumstance and conjuncture, but without denying the vision that makes them revolutionary — and certainly without forsaking revolutionary objectives. Then utopian adventures, inimical to their proponents' intentions, can be avoided and revolutionary undertakings can have some chance of issuing in outcomes consonant with the visions that motivate them. A fundamental task for socialist political theory is therefore to join the rational kernel of the conservative critique of revolutionary politics with a revolutionary determination to push humanity to its limit — 'taking men as they are and laws as they might be'.

I have tried to show how some claims about history and the state of Rousseauean and Marxian provenance provide a sound basis for this project. Like Rousseau, Marx advanced a vision of an ideal order where individuals coordinate behaviour through equal and absolute respect for the autonomy of each person. Marx too envisaged a republic of ends at the end of history. The historical and political theory he developed supports this conclusion. Implicitly, Marx showed how the republic of ends can be more than a moral vision and regulative idea; how it can become a practical political objective.

This book has been a study only in the political theory of the republic of ends. In the exuberant terms of Marx's expression, 'the arm of criticism' does not here pass into 'the criticism of arms'.[1] Nevertheless, there are political purposes served by reflecting on this vision and, more generally, on the possible futures of the socialist state. The present conjuncture makes these purposes urgent.

Needless to say, communism has never had a good press in capitalist countries, and lately even socialism has been put on the defensive in those parts of the capitalist world where it was not already generally despised. However these venerable ideas are crucial for a sustained, progressive politics; not just for the sake of morale in dark times, but for guidance throughout all that remains of the capitalist epoch and, if all goes well, throughout the career of its epochal successor. Progressive forces need a well-grounded vision to direct immediate struggles but also to form longer-range objectives and to shape strategic reflection. Bringing communism back in — and restoring socialism's prestige — is therefore a project of some consequence. This study has been dedicated to this endeavour.

There is also a more immediate objective served by defending the idea of the end of the state and the means for its demise. We have seen how communist statelessness finally instantiates full human freedom; how it can only be the outcome of a protracted revolutionary struggle in and over the state — for its democratization. Democracy is, at once, a necessary means for realizing communism but also, at the limit, communism itself — the earthly organization of the republic of ends. Defending the end of the state is therefore tantamount to defending freedom and democracy and exposing their subversive implications. Both terms have had a long and contested history; both are prone to misappropriation.[2] Freedom has long been invoked in defence of capitalism at the same time that it has motivated progressive, anti-capitalist struggles. Everyone is for freedom, but there is little agreement on what freedom is or what its political implications might be. I would hazard, though, that in the preponderance of cases, 'freedom' has been used against the freedom communism promotes, against autonomy. I fear that 'democracy' now risks a similar fate. In its traditional meaning, the term designated rule by the *demos* — the popular masses. Until the nineteenth century, the consensus view therefore was that democracy was an evil to be avoided. But with the rise of the *demos* in industrial capitalism, the consensus that had dominated political discussion in the West for nearly two thousand years collapsed. In our century, the view has changed completely: as with 'freedom', nearly everyone claims allegiance to 'democracy'. Of course, it is not quite the democracy that was once despised; for one thing, its class content has become obscured. Even so, the term has retained at least a tenuous connection with its original meaning, sufficient for orienting politics generally in the direction of popular empowerment. Now even this connection is in jeopardy.

As these words are written, the government of the world's most powerful and predatory state continues to pursue a global counter-revolutionary policy, now concentrated mainly against the peoples of Central America. It is plain that debasement of political discourse is a concomitant of this strategy and may become its most enduring — and pernicious — legacy. Thugs and mercenaries in the service of the American government and its clients have become 'freedom fighters' and a 'democratic resistance' — in the mouths of functionaries and parliamentarians in nearly all the capitalist states; while a compliant press portrays counter-revolution as a struggle for, of all things, democracy itself. The offence to freedom and democracy — and to the idea of revolution — must not go unchallenged. And neither should progressives tolerate the post-Orwellian machinations of a regime whose hypocrisy, however blatant, is more than usually deadly. It is therefore a task of some moment — along with the evident need to resist the depredations these terms mask — to struggle against this radical misappropriation of language, and to make political discourse honest.

Political philosophy can only be conducted at some remove from actual politics. But insofar as philosophy is a struggle over ideas and words, it has political effects. It is therefore urgent that the struggle be engaged, and that democracy and freedom be wrested away from the barbarians in power and restored to progressive uses. Whatever Marx intended by insisting that 'the arm of criticism' pass into 'the criticism of arms', it is plain that criticism, including analysis and argument, is itself political, and never more than in the present conjuncture. Perhaps at no other time in the history of oppression has the enemy been so dangerous, but also so bankrupt intellectually and therefore so vulnerable to critical assault.

Notes

Preface

1. Cf. J.M. Buchanan, *The Limits of Liberty: Between Anarchy and Leviathan*, University of Chicago Press 1975; and David Gauthier, *Morals By Agreement*, The Clarendon Press 1986.
2. Cf. Donald H. Regan, *Utilitarianism and Co-operation*, The Clarendon Press 1980.
3. Albert O. Hirschman, *Shifting Involvements: Private Interest and Public Action*, Princeton University Press 1982.
4. Andrew Levine, *The Politics of Autonomy: A Kantian Reading of Rousseau's Social Contract*, University of Massachusetts Press 1976.
5. Andrew Levine, *Liberal Democracy: A Critique of Its Theory*, Columbia University Press 1981.
6. Andrew Levine, *Arguing for Socialism: Theoretical Considerations*, Routledge & Kegan Paul 1984.
7. G.A. Cohen, *Karl Marx's Theory of History: A Defense*, Princeton University Press 1978.
8. John Roemer, *A General Theory of Exploitation and Class*, Harvard University Press 1982.

Introduction

1. There are, of course, many imaginable varieties of anarchism. When I speak of anarchism here and in what follows, it should be understood that I intend only those anarchisms — the vast majority — that, like Marxian communism, oppose capitalism.
2. This very inclusive definition will be defended in chapters 5 and 6. See also my *Arguing for Socialism*, op. cit., pp. 5-11.

3. J.-J. Rousseau, *The Social Contract*, Book 1, Introductory Note.
4. Ibid.
5. However, in the Prefatory Note to *The Social Contract* and again in a letter to Moultou, dated 18 January 1762 (in Rousseau, *Oeuvres Completes*, vol. 3, Bibliothèque de la Pléiade 1964, p. 1431), Rousseau notes that *The Social Contract* is an extract from a larger work entitled *Political Institutions*, never completed and now no longer in existence. It may therefore be that in some sense Rousseau regarded normative political philosophy as a kind of prolegomenon to the study of actual politics and not, as the text of *The Social Contract* suggests, an entirely independent enterprise.
6. J.-J. Rousseau, *Discourse on the Origin of Inequality Among Men*, Part 1, Introductory Note.
7. For a recent overview, see Jean-Louis Lecercle, 'Rousseau et Marx' in R.A. Leigh, ed., *Rousseau After Two Hundred Years: Proceedings of the Cambridge Bicentennial Colloquium*, Cambridge University Press 1982.
8. Louis Althusser, 'Rousseau: The Social Contract' in *Politics and History*, New Left Books 1972. The debt is particularly evident in my *The Politics of Autonomy*, op. cit.
9. Galvano Della Volpe, *Rousseau and Marx*, John Fraser, trans., Lawrence and Wishart 1978.
10. Lucio Colletti, *From Rousseau to Lenin: Studies in Ideology and Society*, John Merrington and Judith White, trans., New Left Books 1972.
11. The idea that Rousseau discovered what Kant later went on to elaborate is maintained by Hegel in *The Phenomenology of Spirit* in the section entitled 'The Moral View of the World'. More recently, this claim has been advanced by Ernst Cassirer in a number of texts including *The Question of Jean-Jacques Rousseau*, Peter Gay, trans. and ed., University of Indiana Press 1954; and *Rousseau Kant Goethe*, James Gutmann, P.O. Kristeller and John Herman Randall, Jr., trans. and eds., Princeton University Press 1945. Some of the conceptual affinities joining Rousseau and Kant are elaborated in my *The Politics of Autonomy: A Kantian Reading of Rousseau's 'Social Contract'* op. cit. See also Stephen Ellenburg, 'Rousseau and Kant: Principles of Political Right' in R.A. Leigh, ed., op. cit.
12. Cf. my 'Alienation as Heteronomy', *The Philosophical Forum*, vol. 8, nos 2-4, 1978, pp. 256-68.
13. Cf. Richard W. Miller, 'Marx and Aristotle' in Kai Nielsen and Steven C. Patten, eds., *Marx and Morality, Canadian Journal of Philosophy*, supplementary vol. 7, 1981, pp. 323-52; and Jon Elster, *Making Sense of Marx*, Cambridge University Press 1985, pp. 82-92.
14. To this end, I distinguish a proto-Kantian strain within Rousseau's thought from a distinctly non-Kantian strain; and exhibit their fusion in the appearance of a system. In doing so, I severely qualify the image of a univocal, Kantian Rousseau elaborated in my *The Politics of Autonomy: A Kantian Reading of Rousseau's 'Social Contract'*, op. cit.
15. Here and elsewhere, my use of 'inversion', like my attempts to liberate 'the rational kernel' of this or that from its 'outer polemical shell', should not be construed as an invocation of a 'dialectical' methodology, but as an innocent and playful use of familiar Marxian expressions. By way of precedent, it should be recalled that Marx too admitted in the *Afterward* to the second German edition of *Capital*, volume 1 to 'coquetting' with 'forms of expression peculiar to Hegel'.

Chapter 1

1. Cf. Sergio Cotta, 'La Position du Problème de la Politique Chez Rousseau', *Etudes sur le Contrat Social de Jean-Jacques Rousseau*, Publications de l'Université de Dijon 1964; and Lucio Colletti, 'Rousseau as Critic of Civil Society', in *From Rousseau to Lenin*, op. cit.
2. Liberal democrats characteristically temper this view by adhering simultaneously to the view that individuals ought to control their lives. I have argued elsewhere that, among liberal democrats, this democratic judgement on political institutions is characteristically subordinated to the liberal judgement that individuals are best left free, particularly from political control, to pursue their own affairs in society conceived apart from its political dimensions. I have argued too that liberal and democratic judgements on political institutions coexist in considerable tension — to the detriment of democratic values — and that, in liberal democratic polities, voting and other democratic exercises function more to legitimate prevailing forms of governance than to control them. See my *Liberal Democracy: A Critique of Its Theory*, op. cit.
3. *The Social Contract*, Book 1, chapter 6, Donald A. Cress, trans. and ed., Hackett Publishing Company 1983.
4. *The Social Contract*, Book 4, chapter 2.
5. *The Social Contract*, Book 1, chapter 6.
6. *The Social Contract*, Book 2, chapter 1.
7. For Kant, the material content of the moral order can be discerned, at least in principle, through particular applications of the categorical imperative. For Rousseau, the general interest can be discovered, in principle, by counting the votes. Voting, for Rousseau, is a truth discovery procedure not, as for other democratic theorists, a device for constituting the general will. Cf. my *The Politics of Autonomy*, op. cit., pp. 59-71.
8. Max Weber, 'Politics as a Vocation' in H.H. Gerth and C. Wright Mills, eds., *From Max Weber: Essays in Sociology*, Oxford University Press 1958, p. 78.
9. Cf. my *The Politics of Autonomy*, op. cit., chapter 1.
10. *The Social Contract*, book 1, chapter 6.
11. By 'slavery', Rousseau understands any putative authority relation that fails to regard all parties, including those in subordinate roles, as moral equals. Slavery in this sense is dismissed as a foundation for the *de jure* state in *The Social Contract*, Book 1, chapter 4, precisely because it fails to allow for the realization of autonomy.
12. *The Social Contract*, Book 1, chapter 6.
13. Cf. Ernst Cassirrer, *The Question of Jean-Jacques Rousseau*, op. cit.
14. Cf. The Prelude to Part Two below for discussion of Rousseau's account of the emergence of *amour propre* (rational egoism) out of *amour de soi* (non-acquisitive self-concern) in *The Discourse on the Origin of Inequality Among Men*. For Rousseau, calculations of self-interest determine human actions only after human society comes to be structured by private property. Egoism in the sense in question is therefore not, in Rousseau's view, a feature of human nature as such, but of human nature under determinate social relations.
15. On this point, Rousseau is explicit. See *The Social Contract*, Book 1, chapter 3.

16. This analogy was suggested to me by Joshua Cohen. On pre-commitment and other indirect strategies, see Jon Elster, *Ulysses and the Sirens: Studies in Rationality and Irrationality*, Cambridge University Press 1979; and *Sour Grapes: Studies in the Subversion of Rationality*, Cambridge University Press 1983.

Chapter 2

1. See especially *The Social Contract*, Book 2, chapter 11; *Projet de Constitution pour la Corse* and *Considerations sur le Gouvernement de Pologne* in J.-J. Rousseau, *Oeuvres Completes*, vol. 3, Bibliothèque de la Pléiade 1964.
2. *The Social Contract*, Book 2, chapter 11.
3. See chapter 5 for defence of the definition of capitalism supposed by this description.
4. Ibid. *The Social Contract*, Book 2, chapter 11.
5. Ibid.
6. These claims provide, at best, a *prima facie* case for markets. Among other things, consequences for the freedom, welfare and justice of parties outside particular market transactions must also be taken into account. Cf. my *Arguing for Socialism: Theoretical Considerations*, op. cit. for discussion of these issues.
7. Cf. *The Poltics of Autonomy*, op. cit. chapter 4.
8. See Note 1.
9. *The Emile* and also *La Nouvelle Heloise* provide clear evidence of this retreat. Cf. also Judith N. Shklar, *Men and Citizens: A Study of Rousseau's Social Theory*, Cambridge University Press 1969.
10. I discuss Rousseau's account for government extensively in *The Politics of Autonomy*, op. cit., chapter 3.
11. Cf. *The Social Contract*, Book 2, chapter 7; and *The Politics of Autonomy*, op. cit., pp. 159-67.

Chapter 3

1. *The Correspondence of Edmund Burke*, vol. 6, Cambridge 1971, p. 81. Burke echoes a similar judgement both in his *Reflections on the Revolution in France*, Conor Cruise O'Brien, ed., Penguin 1969, p. 181; and his *Letter to a Member of the National Assembly*, p. 283. In the latter document, Burke suggests that Rousseau would likely dissent from the uses made of his work.
2. *Religion and Philosophy in Germany* (1834), London 1882, p. 106.
3. Quoted by W.J. Bates in his Introduction to *Edmund Burke: Selected Works*, New York 1960, p. 30.
4. Cf. *The Rebel*, London 1962, p. 85ff. Camus wrote (p. 100): 'The very principles of *The Social Contract* presided at the elevation of the tomb which Napoleon Bonaparte came to seal.'
5. Cf. Hannah Arendt, *On Revolution*, New York 1963, p. 75.
6. Cf. J.L. Talmon, *The Origins of Totalitarian Democracy*, New York 1952.

7. Cf. J. Bronowski and Bruce Mazlish, *The Western Intellectual Tradition*, New York 1963.
8. Cf. Daniel Mornet, *Les Origines Intellectuelles de la Revolution Francaise: 1715-1789*, Armand Colin, 6th ed., Paris 1967, pp. 95-6; and also 'L'influence de J.-J. Rousseau au XVIIIeme siecle'. *Annales de la Societe Jean-Jacques Rousseau*, 8, 1912, pp. 33-67.
9. Joan McDonald, *Rousseau and the French Revolution*, London 1965.
10. Cf. George Rude, *Robespierre: Portrait of a Revolutionary Democrat*, Viking Press 1975.
11. M. Robespierre, 'Rapport sur les principes du governement revolutionaire'. *Oeuvres de Maxmilien Robespierre*, vol. 10, Paris 1967, p. 274.
12. M. Robespierre, 'Rapport sur les principes de morale politique qui doivent guider la Convention nationale dans l'administration interieure de la Republique', *Oeuvres*, vol. 10, p. 353.
13. Op. cit., p. 357.
14. See Montesquieu, *The Spirit of the Laws*, Book 2, chapters 3 and 9. Robespierre is perfectly aware of the paradoxical character of this formulation. He had commented on these passages of Montesquieu's two years before in his journal *Le Defenseur de la Constitution*, and the passage just cited continues: 'It has been said that terror was the mainspring of despotic government. Does yours then resemble despotism? Yes, as the sword that glitters in the hands of the heroes of liberty resembles the sword that is wielded by the satellites of tyranny ... The government of the republic is the despotism that liberty exercises against tyranny.'
15. Cf. *The Social Contract*, Book 4, chapter 6. Rousseau's account draws extensively on Machiavelli's views of the dictatorship in ancient Rome in *The Discourses*, Book 1, chapter 34.
16. Ibid.
17. Ibid.
18. Particularly Rousseauean in tone are the debates surrounding the adoption of the Law of 14 Frimaire (December 4 1793) vesting full executive power in the Committees of General Security and Public Safety, thereby suspending the constitution adopted only six months earlier. See, especially, the intervention of Saint-Just, 'Rapport sur la necessité de declarer le gouvernement revolutionnaire jusqu'à la paix', speech of October 10 1793, *Oeuvres de Saint-Just*, Paris 1946, pp. 174-84.
19. By today's standards, the Terror seems relatively mild. Approximately 40,000 people were killed and many more imprisoned or detained. But, of these, the majority of executions took place in the Vendée, Lyons and other provinces in open rebellion. The intensity of the repression varied greatly, coming to a head only at the very end, during the so-called Great Terror of June-July 1794. At all times, the Terror was directed only against individuals in insurrection; never against members of a particular class or race. Needless to say, the twentieth century has produced far greater horrors. But however jaded we may have become, the Terror, in its own time and for a long time afterward, represented the unthinkable itself. Cf. Hegel's understanding of the event in *The Phenomenology of Mind* (C,BB, III), 'Absolute Freedom and Terror'.
20. *The Social Contract*, Book 2, chapter 12. Robespierre echoes these very words: 'What is the end we seek? The peaceful enjoyment of liberty and equality; the reign of that eternal justice whose laws are engraved not on

marble or stone, but in the hearts of men ...' See 'Sur les principes de morale politique', *Oeuvres*, vol. 10, p. 352.

21. Op. cit., book 1, chapter 8.
22. On the notion of virtue in the eighteenth century, see the magisterial study of Robert Mauzi, *L'idée de bonheur au 18e siècle*, Paris 1960, chapter 13. Mauzi concludes: 'On the definition of virtue, the century is unanimous. Virtue consists in according an advantage to the happiness of others over our own happiness. It designates exclusively a social disposition (*aptitude*). Vauvernargues assures us: "The preference for the general interest over the personal is the only definition worthy of virtue and serves to fix the idea." D'Holbach confirms: "Virtue is really only socialibility." Virtue is therefore a subordination (*désaisissement*) of the self for the advantage of others', pp. 580-81.
23. M. Robespierre, 'Sur les principes de morale politique', *Oeuvres*, vol. 10, pp. 353-4. The word *sens* means both 'meaning' and 'direction' or 'tendency'. In both 'senses' the meaning is entirely Rousseauean: the *de jure* state is a form of equality among persons; and it *tends* to create that very equality.
24. On Robiespierre's sympathies for the demands advanced from the bottom of the social order, see A. Manfred, 'La nature du pouvoir jacobin', *La Pensée*, n. 150 (April 1970). It should not be forgotten however, that Robespierre, on a number of occasions, bitterly opposed popular movements particularly the left opposition, the Hebertists, during the period of the Terror. For a more balanced account than Manfred's of Robespierre's social views, see George Rude, *Robespierre: Portrait of a Revolutionary Democrat*, Viking Press 1975, pp. 129-55. There exists a substantial literature attempting, from many different vantage-points, to portray Robespierre as a socialist or proto-socialist. See, for example, Albert Mathiez, 'La corruption parlementaire sous La Terreur', *Etudes Robespierristes*, Paris 1917, pp. 265-93. However, this position is clearly anachronistic and, in any case, socialism is not egalitarianism.
25. See *The Social Contract*, Book 2, chapter 6, where Rousseau advances these claims by insisting that, for an enactment to count as law, it be general in its source and general in its object.
26. It should be evident that, allowance made for the important conceptual differences that distinguish *The Social Contract* from other republican writings — for example, Rousseau's distinction of sovereignty from government — the Rousseauean formulation 'translates' Montesquieu's thesis, cited above [note 14], that virtue is the 'essence'of republican *government.*
27. There is, however, one important exception: government, a partial association necessary for executing the sovereign's will. For discussion of Rousseau's efforts to reconcile the need of government with the need to eliminate partial associations, see *The Politics of Autonomy*, op. cit., pp. 107-13.

Chapter 4

1. For elaboration of this view of politics as an activity and its implications for political theory and practice, cf. Michael Oakeshott, 'Political Education',

in *Rationalism and Politics*, Methuen 1962.

2. Alexis de Tocqueville, *The Old Regime and the French Revolution*, Stuart Gilbert, trans., Doubleday 1955.
3. Op. cit., p. vii.
4. Cf. Alexis de Tocqueville, *Democracy in America*, George Lawrence, trans., New York 1966. Tocqueville's 'liberty' includes Hobbes's freedom (the absence of coercive restraint in the pursuit of one's ends) and also elements of Rousseau's autonomy. In discussing Tocqueville, then, I shall use 'liberty' to refer to his particular understanding of freedom and 'freedom' to designate the senses of freedom with which we are already familiar. Elsewhere, where there is no danger of confusion, I shall use 'liberty' and 'freedom' interchangeably.
5. *The Old Regime and the French Revolution*, p. 137.
6. Cf. op. cit., esp. chapter 3. Also see *Democracy in America*, op. cit.
7. For a different view of the relation between freedom and equality, suggesting a positive correlation, see my *Arguing for Socialism*, op. cit.
8. Edmund Burke, *Reflections on the Revolution in France*, Conor Cruise O'Brien, ed., Penguin 1968.
9. Cf. C.B. Macpherson, *Burke*, Oxford University Press 1980.
10. *Reflections on the Revolution in France*, op. cit., p. 90.
11. Op. cit., pp. 286-87.
12. *The Old Regime and the French Revolution*, op. cit., p. 147.
13. Ibid.
14. Conservatism does not exclude change, but only abrupt and radical change. It would be difficult to imagine a political philosophy that regards change itself as deviant. Certainly neither Burke's nor Tocqueville's does. And though Rousseau, in his Kantian moments, regards the social contract itself as 'eternal' and 'everywhere and always the same', he is intent throughout his political writings to examine the rise and fall of political institutions.
15. Cf. *The Social Contract*, Book 3, chapters 10-15 for Rousseau's account of the inevitable decline of governmental institutions. On the birth of political institutions, cf. *supra* pp. 47-8.
16. These are, of course, only ideological commitments, easily overridden by self-interest. *Laissez-faire* is plainly not a very good way, in most instances, to further business interests, as American liberals long ago realized.
17. More precisely, pre-World War II American conservatism was isolationist with respect to foreign policy towards Europe and its colonies. However interventionism in the western hemisphere and in Asia has a long and unbroken record of support among American conservatives of nearly all varieties.
18. See *The Political Writings of St Augustine*, Henry Paolucci, ed., Gateway 1962. See also Herbert A. Deane, *The Political and Social Ideas of St Augustine*, Columbia University Press 1963.
19. But human beings can, with divine support, organize the maintenance of civil order, the Peace of Babylon, and therefore the governance of political communities. Civil order is a prerequisite for the fulfillment of Providential design in human history; a history structured, in Augustinian theology, by the Fall, the Redemption and, ultimately, the Final Judgement.

Chapter 5

1. See, for instance, the celebrated 1859 Preface to the *Critique of Political Economy.*
2. Cf., among others, G.A. Cohen, *Karl Marx's Theory of History: A Defence*, Oxford 1978, Alan Wood, *Karl Marx*, London 1982, Part 2; William Shaw, *Marx's Theory of History* Standford 1978, and Richard Miller, *Analysing Marx: Morality, Power and History*, Princeton University Press 1984. Cohen's reconstruction and defence of historical materialism is the point of departure for what follows here. See also my *Arguing for Socialism*, op. cit. chapter 6.
3. That Marx was in some sense a technological determinist is a common theme of 'orthodox' Marxian writing on history. See, for instance, Georg Plekhanov, *Fundamental Problems of Marxism*, New York 1969; and *The Development of The Monist View of History*, New York 1972. Marx's technological determinism is a theme of most recent writing on historical materialism. This view has been challenged by Richard Miller, op. cit.
4. An optimizing mechanism is sufficient for insuring directionality, but not necessary. The existence of 'ratchet mechanisms' to prevent backsliding would suffice. Should historical materialism's optimizing claim prove indefensible, therefore, the theory could be modified without altering its distinctive conceptual structure — provided some direction-conferring mechanism is introduced to replace the optimizing mechanism the orthodox theory supposes.
5. Neither is evolutionary theory a teleological theory in the fashion of traditional philosophies of history. It accords no explanatory role to interpretation, and certainly recognizes no analogue to meaning in history.
6. The orthodox theory does not specify the selection mechanism. Thus it has no analogue to the way evolutionary theory can not only compute changes that will occur when selection and other forces act on a population, but can also explain why the ecological circumstances of the population generate a particular array of selection pressures. Historical materialism claims that history has an optimizing property but does not specify what makes this claim true. On this issue, see the exchange between G.A. Cohen and Jon Elster in *Political Studies*, vol. 28, no. 1, 1980.
7. Endogenous here means internal to the system described. Whatever is not endogenous is exogenous. The distinction is theory relative in the sense that it is (Marxian) social theory that tells us that, say, forces of production are endogenous to social systems while climate is not.
8. However even the strictest Darwinians acknowledge endogenous (biological) constraints on change governed by natural selection and other mechanisms operating to accommodate to exogenous factors. What is at issue here, however, are processes that propel change along; not constraints on change.
9. In principle, directionality could also be achieved through (internal) 'ratchet' mechanisms that prevent regression, but do nothing to propel change. Then societies would advance (irreversibly), but not in consequence of internal contradictions or other endogenous, dynamic forces. Historical change would thus resemble learning rather than, as Marx thought, growth.
10. Cf. A. Levine and E.O. Wright, 'Rationality and Class Struggle', *New Left*

Review, no. 123, 1980; and A. Levine, *Arguing for Socialism: Theoretical Considerations*, Routledge & Kegan Paul 1984.

11. Cf. Levine, op. cit.
12. See, for example, Theda Skocpol, *States and Social Revolution*, Cambridge University Press 1979, for some suggestions to this effect.
13. Cf. G.A. Cohen, 'Inclusive and Restricted Historical Materialism', forthcoming.
14. See, for example, Etienne Balibar, 'The Fundamental Concepts of Historical Materialism', in L. Althusser and E. Balibar, *Reading Capital*, New Left Books 1971.
15. 'Materialism' in this context is a view about the nature of social causality. For a materialist, the pertinent social causes are material — that is, technological and also, in Balibar's case, economic — as opposed to ideal factors, such as values or norms. A materialist sociology, then, is a sociology that explains by reference to material causes.

Chapter 6

1. Marx seems to have believed that historical materialism provides, at least in principle, an account of transitions between pre-capitalist economic structures. Cf. Karl Marx, *Grundrisse: Introduction to the Critique of Political Economy*, Martin Nicolaus, trans., Penugin 1973, pp. 471-514. In G.A. Cohen's reconstruction of the orthodox view, this claim is expressly denied. Historical materialism, for Cohen, provides an account just of the transition from pre-capitalist class societies to capitalism, but not between pre-capitalist class societies. Cf. G.A. Cohen, op. cit., pp. 197-201. If Cohen is right, it may be, in part, for the reason just indicated: that pre-capitalist class societies do not comprise distinct natural kinds. The term 'pre-capitalist class society' would then designate a natural kind that admits of many variants distinguished by different forms of private property in persons.
2. The idea is commonly — and correctly — associated with John Locke, but was by no means exclusive to him. Cf. C.B. Macpherson, *The Political Theory of Possessive Individualism: Hobbes to Locke*, Oxford University Press 1962, chapter 3.
3. See my *Arguing for Socialism*, op. cit., pp. 5-11.
4. Cf. Nancy Holmstrom, 'Exploitation', *Canadian Journal of Philosophy*, vol. 7, no. 2, June 1977; and Jeffrey Reiman, 'Exploitation, Force, and the Moral Assessment of Capitalism: Thoughts on Roemer and Cohen', *Philosophy and Public Affairs*, forthcoming.
5. By focusing just on the distributive implications of exploitation relations, it can be argued that exploitation is not, in fact, morally objectionable. Cf. John Roemer, 'Should Marxists Be Interested in Exploitation?' *Philosophy and Public Affairs* vol. 14, 1985, pp. 30-65. Roemer endorses this unlikely conclusion, but see the rejoinder by Reimann, op. cit.
6. Cf., among others, John Roemer, *A General Theory of Exploitation and Class*, Harvard University Press 1982; and Robert Paul Wolff, *Understanding Marx*, Princeton University Press 1984. What follows draws on my *Arguing for Socialism*, op. cit., pp. 65-76.

7. Cf. John Roemer, op. cit.
8. For a discussion of some difficulties with Roemer's game theoretic approach in other contexts, see Jon Elster, 'Roemer versus Roemer: A Comment on "New Directions in the Marxian Theory of Exploitation and Class"', and Roemer's 'Reply' in *Politics and Society*, vol. 11, no. 3, 1982. Needless to say, this purchase on exploitation focuses exclusively on its distributional implications and is therefore inadequate for grasping the sense in which exploitation is an evil. In 'Should Marxists Be Interested in Exploitation', Roemer identifies this inadequacy perspicuously, but oddly with a view to minimizing the importance of exploitation as a critical concept. Cf. note 5.
9. Cf. John Roemer, 'New Directions in the Marxian Theory of Exploitation and Class', *Politics and Society*, vol. 11, no. 3, 1982.
10. Cf. my 'Towards Marxian Justice', in *Politics and Society*, op. cit.
11. Cf. *The Critique of the Gotha Programme* in Marx, Engels, *Collected Works*, vol. 2, Moscow 1962, p. 24.
12. Ibid.
13. This is not to say that inequalities resulting from differential expenditures of effort, freely undertaken, are beyond reproach. One might object, for instance, on grounds of equality, considered as an end-in-itself. Thus even 'deserved' inequalities might be thought objectionable.
14. Similarly, it is not obvious that remuneration between relatively well-off and relatively poorly-off communities should be equalized. More would need to be said about how the existing distribution came about. Similar considerations apply across sectors within communities. To the degree resources are distributed unequally in consequence of past efforts, there is apparently no injustice in enjoying the fruits of these efforts.
15. Cf. *Arguing for Socialism*, op. cit., pp. 65-76 for arguments to this effect.
16. John Roemer, 'New Directions in the Marxian Theory of Exploitation and Class', op. cit., p. 283.
17. Cf. Erik Olin Wright, *Classes*, Verso 1985, chapter 2.
18. See, for instance, Etienne Balibar, *On the Dictatorship of the Proletariat*, New Left Books 1977 and my 'Balibar on the Dictatorship of the Proletariat', *Politics and Society*, vol. 7, no. 1, 1977, pp. 69-84.
19. *The Social Contract*, Book 1, chapter 8.
20. Karl Marx, Frederick Engels, *Collected Works*, vol. 3, International Publishers 1975.
21. Cf. my 'Alienation as Heteronomy', *Philosophical Forum*, vol. 8, nos. 2-4, 1978, pp. 256-68.
22. On Marx's identification of 'communism' with the end of alienation, see Stanley Moore, *Marx on the Choice Between Socialism and Communism*, Harvard University Press 1980. esp. pp. 8-18.
23. Cf. my 'Althusser's Marxism', *Economy and Society*, vol. 10, no. 3, 1981. There plainly are important conceptual discontinuities in the Marxian corpus, though it is easy, as Althusser's case attests, to overstate discontinuities for polemical purposes. Still, the 'epistemological break' Althusser identified is there: Marx practiced and then, around 1845, abandoned philosophical anthropology of the Feuerbachian sort. The abandonment, however, was never complete and certainly not so self-conscious as Marx himself asserted, for instance, in the *Theses on Feuerbach* and *The German Ideology*.

24. Cf. *Liberal Democracy*, op. cit., chapter 2.
25. 'Constant capital' designates investment in machinery and other alienable means of production; 'variable capital' designates investment in labour inputs. The organic composition of capital rises, in the traditional view, because each capitalist firm, to survive the competition of capitalist markets, must invest in fixed capital to improve the productivity of its workers. In value theoretic terms, increasing investments in fixed capital augments the rate of exploitation, the ratio of surplus value to variable capital. Since, in Marx's view, exploitation is the basis for profits, an increasing rate of exploitation is generally realized in increased profits. It is, of course, the search for profits that motivates capitalist investment. Capitalists therefore have an incentive to invest, at the same time that their investments collectively undermine the conditions that make investments worthwhile. Capitalist enterprises, in other words, are in a situation where, in the long run, individual optimizing behaviour works to the detriment of everyone.
26. Cf., among others, Robert Paul Wolff, *Understanding Marx: A Reconstruction and Critique of Capital*, Princeton University Press 1984; John Roemer, *Analytical Foundations of Marxian Economic Theory*, Cambridge University Press 1981; and Jon Elster, *Making Sense of Marx*, Cambridge University Press 1985, pp. 119-165.
27. Cf. G.A. Cohen, op. cit., pp. 193-215 and 302-7. In traditional Marxian political economy, the tendency of the rate of profit to fall is only one of a number of endogenous causes of crises. Also important are cyclical phenomena of under-consumption and over-production. In Cohen's view, these cyclical phenomena do persist and even intensify in late capitalism. Their persistence, in fact, is an important element in the story he tells to explain the effective emergence of an interest in moving from capitalism to socialism on the part of workers and their potential allies.
28. Cf. Philippe Van Parijs and Robert Van der Veen, 'The Capitalist Road to Communism', forthcoming in *Theory and Society*.
29. See my *Arguing for Socialism*, op. cit.
30. Op. cit., chapter 3.
31. Cf. Alec Nove, *The Economics of Feasible Socialism*, Allen and Unwin 1983.
32. Cf. Robert Nozick in *Anarchy, State, Utopia*, Basic Books 1974, chapter 7, esp. pp. 160-3.
33. Capitalist societies typically proscribe pre-capitalist social relations — for instance, pacts of slavery or fealty — to the dismay of hardly anyone except doctrinaire libertarians. But slavery and feudalism appear to have exhausted their attraction in a way that capitalism has not. That a person is prohibited from becoming a slave or a serf does not seem nowadays to detract at all from his or her freedom. However a prohibition against starting one's own business would.

Chapter 7

1. Cf. chapters 1 and 2, upon which the discussion here draws.
2. Cf., *inter alia*, *The Social Contract*, Book 4, chapter 1.

3. Cf. chapter 6.
4. Cf. especially, Karl Marx, 'The Civil War in France', and V.I. Lenin, *The State and Revolution, Collected Works*, vol. 25, Progress Publishers 1964.
5. Cf. *The Social Contract*, Book 2, chapter 6.
6. Cf. 'Politics as a Vocation' in H.H. Gerth and C. Wright Mills eds., *From Max Weber: Essays in Sociology*, Oxford University Press 1958, p. 78.
7. Cf. chapter 1.
8. These positions, though clarified and 'corrected' by Marx and Engels throughout their political writings — above all, in view of the experience of the Paris Commune of 1871 — are evident in the Marxian corpus at least from the time, just prior to the 1848 Revolutions, of *The Communist Manifesto.* See Etienne Balibar, 'La Rectification du "Manifeste Communiste"', in *Cinq Etudes du Materialisme Historique*, Maspero 1974.
9. Cf. *supra*, chapter 1.
10. On Marx's uses of 'dictatorship', see Elster op. cit., pp, 447-49 and Hal Draper, 'Marx and the Dictatorship of the Proletariat', *Etudes de Marxologie* 6, 1962, *Cahiers de l'ISEA*, no. 129, pp. 5-74.
11. Thomas Hobbes, *Leviathan*, Michael Oakeshott, ed., Basil Blackwell, n.d., chapter 13.
12. The relative equality of individuals' power is a consequence of the relatively equal distribution of physical and mental endowments in what would today be called the natural lottery. With very few exceptions, human beings in a state of nature are sufficiently equal in mental and physical endowments that they can — by themselves or in temporary coalition with others — do each other mortal harm. Everyone is vulnerable to the assaults of everyone else. It is, in part, for this reason that it is rational to try to cooperate, 'to seek peace and follow it'.
13. Cf. Etienne Balibar, *On the Dictatorship of the Proletariat*, New Left Books 1977.
14. Cf. *supra*, chapter 6.
15. Cf., *inter alia*, Alec Nove in *The Economics of Feasible Socialism*, op. cit., pp. 55-60.
16. Cf. V.I. Lenin, *The State and Revolution, Collected Works*, vol. 25, Progress Publishers 1954.
17. Cf. *supra*, chapter 6.
18. Arguably, the prolonging of revolutionary Terror, long after it had lost any plausible rationale, is among the more important reasons why the revolution the Bolsheviks launched failed to move in a communist direction.
19. Cf. *supra*, chapter 3.
20. Cf. Elster, op. cit., pp. 408-11; and Ralph Miliband, *Marxism and Politics*, Oxford University Press 1977.
21. The canonical text in this regard is, of course, *The Eighteenth Brumaire of Louis Napoleon.* On Marx's post-1871 non-instrumentalism, cf. Etienne Balibar, 'La Rectification du "Manifeste Communiste"', op. cit.
22. An increasing awareness of the state in a world system of states — and indeed of national, capitalist economies in a world capitalist system — has given increased impetus to claims for state autonomy. Thus 'world systems theory' has become a powerful force within and at the margins of Marxian historical and sociological research. Its founding texts are Immanuel Wallerstein, *The Modern World System. Capitalist Agriculture and the Origins of the European World-Economy in the Sixteenth Century*, Aca-

demic Press 1974; and 'The Rise and Future Demise of the Capitalist World System: Concepts for Comparative Analysis', *Comparative Studies in Society and History* vol. 16 September 1974, pp. 187-415. Insofar as states do more than superintend economic relations within given polities, but also conduct affairs between polities in ways that structure economic relations, it is implausible to suppose that their internal, domestic functions exclusively shape their character and capacities. Cf. Nora Hamilton, *The Limits of State Autonomy: Post-Revolutionary Mexico*, Princeton University Press 1982.
23. Cf. chapter 6.
24. Cf. *supra* Chapter 6.
25. Cf. *supra*, Chapter 6.
26. It has become commonplace to use the term 'existing socialism' to refer to the political economic system in place in the Soviet Union and other Communist countries. In contrast to many writers, my use of the term is not at all ironic.

Chapter 8

1. *The Social Contract*, Book 1, chapter 6.
2. Thus one could imagine an account of peace between nations that appeals not to any diminution in a disposition to war, but to the achievement of a balance of power between belligerent states. For a Hobbesian theory of international relations, actual peace would be a consequence of objective conditions different from those pertaining in the state of nature. There would be no analogue, strictly speaking, to the relative equality of persons.
3. Cf. Prelude to Part 2.
4. But, as we know (see chapter 1), *amour propre* threatens essential humanity. Paradoxically, then, what distinguishes human beings from animals actually, i.e. empirically, threatens to undo what distinguishes human beings notionally.
5. Cf. Prelude to Part 2 and chapter 5.
6. Games of this sort are called Prisoners' Dilemmas because of a story sometimes told to motivate the assignment of pay-offs. Imagine a prosecuting lawyer making a deal with each of two prisoners, Tom and Harry, who can either confess or not confess to some crime. Each is told that if he confesses and his partner doesn't, he can go free while his partner will face a twenty-year jail sentence. If they both confess, they will each go to jail but for only eight years. If neither confesses, there is evidence enough to convict each only for some minor offence, carrying a three-year sentence. Thus the pay-off matrix conforms to the Prisoners' Dilemma structure:

		Harry	
		confesses	doesn't confess
Tom	confesses	−8,−8	0,−20
	doesn't confess	−20,0	−3,−3

For reasons already rehearsed, the prisoners will each confess and the outcome for each will be worse than it would have been, had they not confessed. The Prisoners' Dilemma is attributed to A.W. Tucker and has been much discussed and employed since its discovery in the 1950s. This literature is extensively reviewed in Anatol Rapoport and A.M. Chammah, *Prisoners' Dilemma: A Study in Conflict and Cooperation*, University of Michigan Press 1965; and Russell Hardin, *Collective Action*, The Johns Hopkins University Press 1982.

7. In these circumstances, the ideal situation for any particular individual is to be a lone disobedient, defecting while everyone else cooperates. In the standard contractarian view, each individual prefers lone disobedience to general cooperation, and general cooperation to the war of all against all. However lone disobedience, as a collective policy, is logically impossible. In a world of defectors, there would be no cooperation and, therefore, no lone disobedience. If the most preferred alternative were generally adopted, the least preferred alternative, the war of all against all, would result. Cf. David Lewis, *Convention: A Philosophical Study* Harvard University Press 1969.
8. Cf. *The Social Contract*, Book 1, chapter 6.
9. Cf. chapter 7.
10. Rousseau, unlike Hobbes, thought geographical proximity socially produced. In the early state of nature, described in *The Second Discourse*, individuals lived in virtual isolation, coming together only briefly and occasionally — mainly to procreate. It is the technological innovations that made settled agriculture possible that form the basis, in Rousseau's view, for population increases — making geographical proximity a fact of the human condition.
11. Cf. Robert Axelrod, *The Evolution of Cooperation*, Basic Books 1984.
12. Cf. *The Social Contract*, Book 2, chapter 11 and the discussion here in chapter 2.
13. Cf. *The Critique of the Gotha Program, Collected Works*, vol. 2, op. cit.
14. Cf. Allen E. Buchanan, 'The Marxian Critique of Justice and Rights' in Kai Nielsen and Steven C. Patten eds., *Marx and Morality*, supplementary vol. 7 of *The Canadian Journal of Philosophy*, 1981.
15. The Soviet system of delegation, and its analogues in nearly all revolutionary undertakings since the Paris Commune, are (spontaneous) approximations of Rousseauean direct democracy, suited to political communities too large and complex for the entire people to be assembled for debate and collective choice. The Paris Commune and its successors are, in a sense, approximations of *The Social Contract's* approximation of the republic of ends.
16. Cf. chapter 7.
17. Op. cit.
18. Cf. *Arguing for Socialism*, op. cit. pp. 217-25.
19. Cf. *Arguing for Socialism*, op. cit.
20. Cf. Introduction.
21. Cf. chapter 2.
22. I discuss Rousseau's account of government extensively in *The Politics of Autonomy*, op. cit., pp. 107-58.

Conclusion

1. Cf. 'Introduction to *The Critique of Hegel's Philosophy of Right*', in Marx, Engels, *Collected Works*, vol. 4.
2. Cf. my *Arguing for Socialism*, op. cit. for amplification of the assertions that follow.

Index

Althusser, L., 13, 183, 191
Alienation, 122
Analytical Marxism, 6-7
Anarchism, 9, 18, 136-144, 169-175
Arendt, H., 50
Aristotle, 26
Augustine, 26-7, 71, 73, 82-84, 88, 173, 188-189
Autonomy, 14, 121-125, 168, 180

Balibar, E., 191, 193
Bodin, J., 32
Bolshevism, 136-144, 170
Bronowski, J., 51
Buchanan, A.E., 195
Buchanan, J.M., 182
Burke, E., 15, 21, 50, 70-79, 169, 174

Camus, A., 50
Capitalism, 41-45, 106-110, 122-130
Cassirer, E., 184
Chamma, A., 195
Civil Religion, 46, 63
Classes and Classlessness, *passim.*
Cohen, G.A., 6, 93-104, 182, 189, 192
Cohen, J., 185
Colletti, L., 13
Communism, 9-13, 121-130, 154-175
Comte, A., 88
Conservatism, 69-72, 80-84
Cotta, S., 184

Darwinism, 93-101, 104, 163, 189
Della Volpe, G., 13
Democracy, 131-136, 169-175, 180
Descartes, R., 70-71
Dictatorship, (in Rousseau) 53-57, (of the Proletariat) 18, 136-153, 169-175
Discourse on the Origin of Inequality, 87-91, 183

Ecological movement, 3-4
Elster, J., 185, 189
Engels, F., 13, 173-175
Evolutionary Biology, 93-101
Existing Socialism, 114-130
Exploitation, 110-121

Feuerbachian humanism, 14
Feminism, 4-6

Gauthier, D., 182

Hamilton, N., 194
Hardin, R., 195
Hegel, G.W.F., 14, 88, 183, 186
Heine, H., 50
Hirschman, A.O., 182

Hobbes, T., 1-3, 27, 29-38, 71, 73, 82-84, 138-139, 155-164, 171, 178, 193
Holmstrom, N., 191

Jacobinism, 50-66, 67-69

Kant I., 1-4, 25-38, 88, 167-175, 184

Lawgiver, 47-48
Lenin, V.I., 15, 131-134, 170-175, 193
Lewis, D., 195

Macchiavelli, N., 32, 138
McDonald, J., 51
Manfred, A., 187
Marx, K., *passim.*
Mathiez, A., 187
Mauzi, R., 187
Mazlich, B., 51
Miller, R.W., 183
Moeurs., 45-49, 148
Montesquieu, C., 186, 187
Moral recalcitrance, 34-36
Mornet, D., 51

Nove, A., 192
Nozick, R., 126, 192

Oakeshott, M., 188
The Old Regime and the French Revolution, 72-74

Prisoners' Dilemma, 139, 155-169, 194

Rapoport, A., 195
Reflections on the Revolution in France, 74-76
Regan, D.H., 182
Revolution, 10-11
Robespierre, M., 15, 50-66, 187
Roemer, J., 6, 111-121, 182, 191, 192
Rousseau, J.-J. *passim.*
Rude, George, 187

Saint-Simon, 13, 173-175
Self-realization, 14
Shaw, W., 189
The Social Contract, passim.
Socialism, *passim.*
Spengler, O., 88
State Autonomy, 144-153
The State and Revolution, 170-171

Talmon, J.L., 50
Teleological Philosophies of History, 88-89
Terror, 55-57
Tocqueville, A. de, 15, 21, 70-79, 169, 174, 188
Tucker, A.W., 195

Van der Veen, R., 192
Van Parijs, P., 192
Virtue, 57-59

Wallerstein, I., 194
Weak Historical Materialism, 101-104
Weber, M., 138, 184
Wolff, R.P., 191
Women's Movement, 4-6
Wood, A., 189
Wright, E.O., 190, 191

9 780860 918813

Printed and bound by CPI Group (UK) Ltd, Croydon, CR0 4YY

06/07/2026

02160637-0001